Reading and Note Taking Guide
Level A

California
Focus on **Earth** *Science*

PEARSON
Education

To the Teacher

This Reading and Note Taking Guide helps your students succeed in their study of science. Working through the exercises will help them understand and organize the concepts presented in the textbook. The completed worksheets then become easy-to-follow study guides for test preparation.

This Reading and Note Taking Guide also helps students improve their study and reading skills. The section "Your Keys to Success" on pages 5–10 of this Guide describes English/Language Arts skills developed in the textbook. Distribute copies of this section for students to use as a reference when completing the worksheets. Students will find it a handy tool for becoming successful readers in science and other subjects.

Cover Images: Prentice Hall Poppy, Foreground r, Corbis; **Poppy,** Foreground r, Charles O'Rear/Corbis; **Poppy Field,** Ralph A. Clevenger/Corbis.
Scott Foresman Front cover, bluestripe snapper, Dave Fleetham/Pacific Stock; **background,** coral reef, coral detail, Stuart Westmorland/Corbis. **Back Cover, top,** DK images; **middle,** Bruce Davidson/Nature Picture Library; **bottom,** Cameron/Corbis; **background coral detail,** Stuart Westmorland/Corbis.

Pearson Prentice Hall™ is a trademark of Pearson Education, Inc.
Pearson® is a registered trademark of Pearson plc.
Prentice Hall® is a registered trademark of Pearson Education, Inc.

Pearson Prentice Hall ISBN-13: 978-0-13-203438-8
Pearson Prentice Hall ISBN-10: 0-13-203438-7

14 15   V011   12 11 10

Pearson Scott Foresman ISBN-13: 978-0-328-26196-3
Pearson Scott Foresman ISBN-10: 0-328-26196-3

11 12 13 14 15 -V011- 14 13 12 11 10

Contents
Earth Science

Your Keys to Success

How to Read Science

Reading Skill The target reading skills introduced on this page will help you read and understand information in this textbook. Each chapter introduces a reading skill. Developing these reading skills is key to becoming a successful reader in science and other subject areas.

Preview Text Structure By understanding how textbooks are organized, you can gain information from them more effectively. This textbook is organized with red headings and blue subheadings. Before you read, preview the headings. Ask yourself questions to guide you as you read. (Chapter 1)

Preview Visuals The visuals in your science textbook provide important information. Visuals are photographs, graphs, tables, diagrams, and illustrations. Before you read, take the time to preview the visuals in a section. Look closely at the title, labels, and captions. Then ask yourself questions about the visuals. (Chapter 2)

Sequence Many parts of a science textbook are organized by sequence. Sequence is the order in which a series of events occurs. Some sections may discuss events in a process that has a beginning and an end. Other sections may describe a continuous process that does not have an end. (Chapters 3 and 10)

Compare and Contrast Science texts often make comparisons. When you compare and contrast, you examine the similarities and differences between things. You can compare and contrast by using a table or a Venn diagram. (Chapters 8 and 12)

Identify Main Ideas As you read, you can understand a section or paragraph more clearly by finding the main idea. The main idea is the most important idea. The details in a section or paragraph support the main idea. Headings and subheadings can often help you identify the main ideas. (Chapters 5 and 11)

Identify Supporting Evidence Science textbooks often describe the scientific evidence that supports a theory or hypothesis. Scientific evidence includes data and facts, information whose accuracy can be confirmed by experiments or observation. A hypothesis is a possible explanation for observations made by scientists or an answer to a scientific question. (Chapter 4)

Create Outlines You can create outlines to help you clarify the text. An outline shows the relationship between main ideas and supporting details. Use the text structure—headings, subheadings, key concepts, and key terms— to help you figure out information to include in your outline. (Chapter 6 and 9)

Take Notes Science chapters are packed with information. Taking good notes is one way to help you remember key ideas and to see the big picture. When you take notes, include key ideas, a few details, and summaries. (Chapter 7)

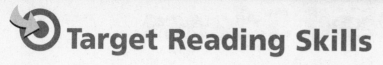

Target Reading Skills

Each chapter provides a target reading skill with clear instruction to help you read and understand the text. You will apply the skill as you read. Then you will record what you've learned in the section and chapter assessments.

Before You Read

Each chapter introduces a target reading skill and provides examples and practice exercises.

As You Read

As you read, you can use the target reading skill to help you increase your understanding.

After You Read

You can apply the target reading skill in the Section Assessments and in the Chapter Assessments.

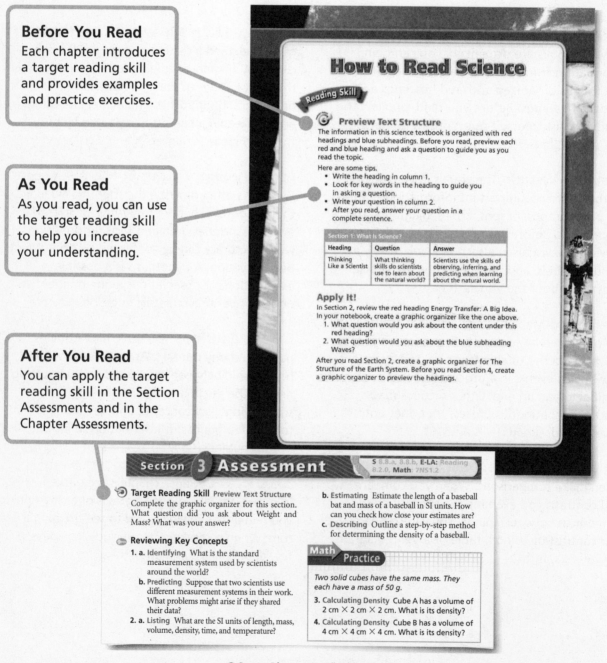

How to Read Science

Reading Skill

Preview Text Structure

The information in this science textbook is organized with red headings and blue subheadings. Before you read, preview each red and blue heading and ask a question to guide you as you read the topic.

Here are some tips.
- Write the heading in column 1.
- Look for key words in the heading to guide you in asking a question.
- Write your question in column 2.
- After you read, answer your question in a complete sentence.

Section 1: What Is Science?		
Heading	**Question**	**Answer**
Thinking Like a Scientist	What thinking skills do scientists use to learn about the natural world?	Scientists use the skills of observing, inferring, and predicting when learning about the natural world.

Apply It!

In Section 2, review the red heading Energy Transfer: A Big Idea. In your notebook, create a graphic organizer like the one above.
1. What question would you ask about the content under this red heading?
2. What question would you ask about the blue subheading Waves?

After you read Section 2, create a graphic organizer for The Structure of the Earth System. Before you read Section 4, create a graphic organizer to preview the headings.

Section 3 Assessment

S 8.8.a, 8.8.b, **E-LA:** Reading 8.2.0, **Math:** 7NS1.2

Target Reading Skill Preview Text Structure
Complete the graphic organizer for this section. What question did you ask about Weight and Mass? What was your answer?

Reviewing Key Concepts

1. a. Identifying What is the standard measurement system used by scientists around the world?
   b. Predicting Suppose that two scientists use different measurement systems in their work. What problems might arise if they shared their data?

2. a. Listing What are the SI units of length, mass, volume, density, time, and temperature?

b. Estimating Estimate the length of a baseball bat and mass of a baseball in SI units. How can you check how close your estimates are?

c. Describing Outline a step-by-step method for determining the density of a baseball.

Math Practice

Two solid cubes have the same mass. They each have a mass of 50 g.

3. Calculating Density Cube A has a volume of 2 cm × 2 cm × 2 cm. What is its density?

4. Calculating Density Cube B has a volume of 4 cm × 4 cm × 4 cm. What is its density?

Build Science Vocabulary

Studying science involves learning a new vocabulary. Here are some vocabulary skills to help you learn the meaning of words you do not recognize.

Word Analysis You can use your knowledge of word parts—prefixes, suffixes, and roots—to determine the meaning of unfamiliar words.

Prefixes A prefix is a word part that is added at the beginning of a root or base word to change its meaning. Knowing the meaning of prefixes will help you figure out new words. You will practice this skill in Chapter 12.

Suffixes A suffix is a letter or group of letters added to the end of a word to form a new word with a slightly different meaning. Adding a suffix to a word often changes its part of speech. You will practice this skill in Chapter 2.

Word Origins Many science words come to English from other languages, such as Greek and Latin. By learning the meaning of a few common Greek and Latin roots, you can determine the meaning of new science words. You will practice this skill in Chapters 3, 4, and 7.

Use Clues to Determine Meaning When you come across a word you don't recognize in science texts, you can use context clues to figure out what the word means. First look for clues in the word itself. Then look at the surrounding words, sentences, and paragraphs for clues. You will practice this skill in Chapter 6.

Identify Multiple Meanings To understand science concepts, you must use terms precisely. Some familiar words may have different meanings in science. Watch for these multiple-meaning words as you read. You will practice this skill in Chapter 8.

Identify Related Word Forms You can increase your vocabulary by learning related forms of words or word families. If you know the meaning of a verb form, you may be able to figure out the related noun and adjective forms. You will practice this skill in Chapter 10.

atmos + sphaira = atmosphere
vapor   sphere   a layer of
gas   vapor or
                                 gases that
                                 surrounds
                                 Earth

Vocabulary Skills

One of the important steps in reading this science textbook is to be sure that you understand the key terms. Your book shows several strategies to help learn important vocabulary.

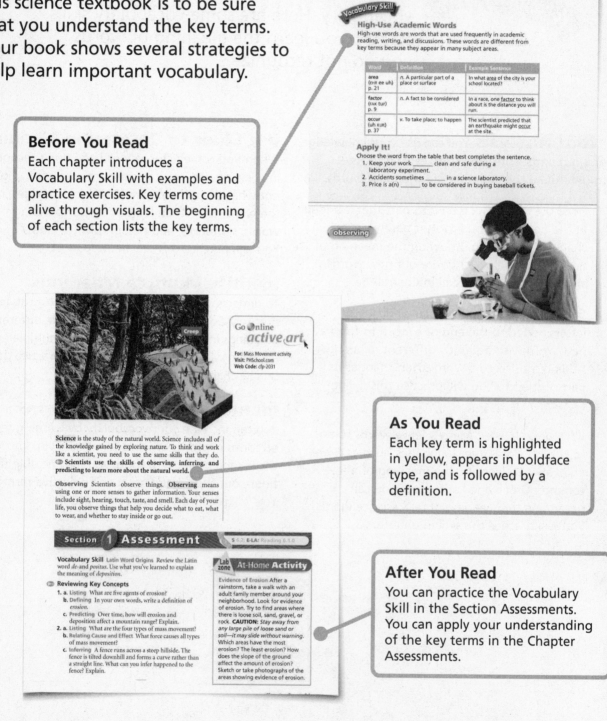

Build Science Vocabulary

The images shown here represent some of the key terms in this chapter. You can use this vocabulary skill to help you understand the meaning of some key terms in this chapter.

Vocabulary Skill

High-Use Academic Words
High-use words are words that are used frequently in academic reading, writing, and discussions. These words are different from key terms because they appear in many subject areas.

Word	Definition	Example Sentence
area (EHR ee uh) p. 21	n. A particular part of a place or surface	In what area of the city is your school located?
factor (FAK tur) p. 9	n. A fact to be considered	In a race, one factor to think about is the distance you will run.
occur (uh KUR) p. 37	v. To take place; to happen	The scientist predicted that an earthquake might occur at the site.

Apply It!
Choose the word from the table that best completes the sentence.
1. Keep your work _____ clean and safe during a laboratory experiment.
2. Accidents sometimes _____ in a science laboratory.
3. Price is a(n) _____ to be considered in buying baseball tickets.

observing

Before You Read

Each chapter introduces a Vocabulary Skill with examples and practice exercises. Key terms come alive through visuals. The beginning of each section lists the key terms.

Creep

Go Online
active art

For: Mass Movement activity
Visit: PHSchool.com
Web Code: cfp-2031

Science is the study of the natural world. Science includes all of the knowledge gained by exploring nature. To think and work like a scientist, you need to use the same skills that they do. Scientists use the skills of observing, inferring, and predicting to learn more about the natural world.

Observing Scientists observe things. **Observing** means using one or more senses to gather information. Your senses include sight, hearing, touch, taste, and smell. Each day of your life, you observe things that help you decide what to eat, what to wear, and whether to stay inside or go out.

As You Read

Each key term is highlighted in yellow, appears in boldface type, and is followed by a definition.

Section 1 Assessment   S 6.2; E-LA: Reading 6.1.0

Vocabulary Skill Latin Word Origins Review the Latin word *de-* and *positus*. Use what you've learned to explain the meaning of *deposition*.

Reviewing Key Concepts
1. a. Listing What are five agents of erosion?
   b. Defining In your own words, write a definition of *erosion*.
   c. Predicting Over time, how will erosion and deposition affect a mountain range? Explain.
2. a. Listing What are the four types of mass movement?
   b. Relating Cause and Effect What force causes all types of mass movement?
   c. Inferring A fence runs across a steep hillside. The fence is tilted downhill and forms a curve rather than a straight line. What can you infer happened to the fence? Explain.

Lab zone At-Home Activity

Evidence of Erosion After a rainstorm, take a walk with an adult family member around your neighborhood. Look for evidence of erosion. Try to find areas where there is loose soil, sand, gravel, or rock. CAUTION: Stay away from any large pile of loose sand or soil—it may slide without warning. Which areas have the most erosion? The least erosion? How does the slope of the ground affect the amount of erosion? Sketch or take photographs of the areas showing evidence of erosion.

After You Read

You can practice the Vocabulary Skill in the Section Assessments. You can apply your understanding of the key terms in the Chapter Assessments.

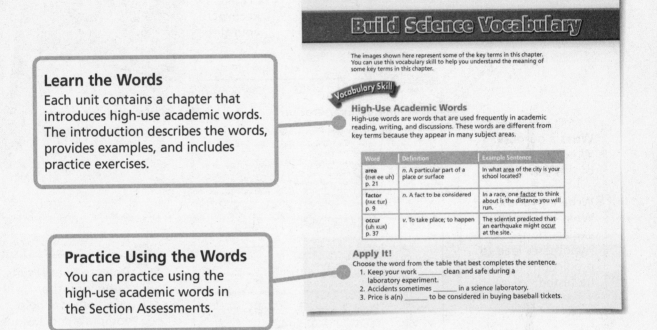

Build Science Vocabulary

High-Use Academic Words

High-use academic words are words that are used frequently in classroom reading, writing, and discussions. They are different from key terms because they appear in many subject areas.

Build Science Vocabulary

The images shown here represent some of the key terms in this chapter. You can use this vocabulary skill to help you understand the meaning of some key terms in this chapter.

Vocabulary Skill

High-Use Academic Words

High-use words are words that are used frequently in academic reading, writing, and discussions. These words are different from key terms because they appear in many subject areas.

Word	Definition	Example Sentence
area (EHR ee uh) p. 21	n. A particular part of a place or surface	In what area of the city is your school located?
factor (FAK tur) p. 9	n. A fact to be considered	In a race, one factor to think about is the distance you will run.
occur (uh KUR) p. 37	v. To take place; to happen	The scientist predicted that an earthquake might occur at the site.

Apply It!

Choose the word from the table that best completes the sentence.
1. Keep your work _____ clean and safe during a laboratory experiment.
2. Accidents sometimes _____ in a science laboratory.
3. Price is a(n) _____ to be considered in buying baseball tickets.

Learn the Words

Each unit contains a chapter that introduces high-use academic words. The introduction describes the words, provides examples, and includes practice exercises.

Practice Using the Words

You can practice using the high-use academic words in the Section Assessments.

Focus on Earth Science High-Use Academic Words

Learning the meaning of these words will help you improve your reading comprehension in all subject areas.

alter	contribute	feature	physical	reverse
area	convert	function	positive	series
category	define	generate	predictable	source
channel	detect	indicate	principle	structure
concept	distinct	individual	process	sustain
conduct	diversity	interpret	proportion	technique
constant	enable	layer	range	theory
construct	environment	major	region	transfer
consumer	estimate	method	reject	trigger
contact	expand	obtain	release	uniform
contract	exposure	occur	remove	vary
contrast	factor	percent	resource	

Investigations

You can explore the concepts in this textbook through inquiry. Like a real scientist, you can develop your own scientific questions and perform labs and activities to find answers. Follow the steps below when doing a lab.

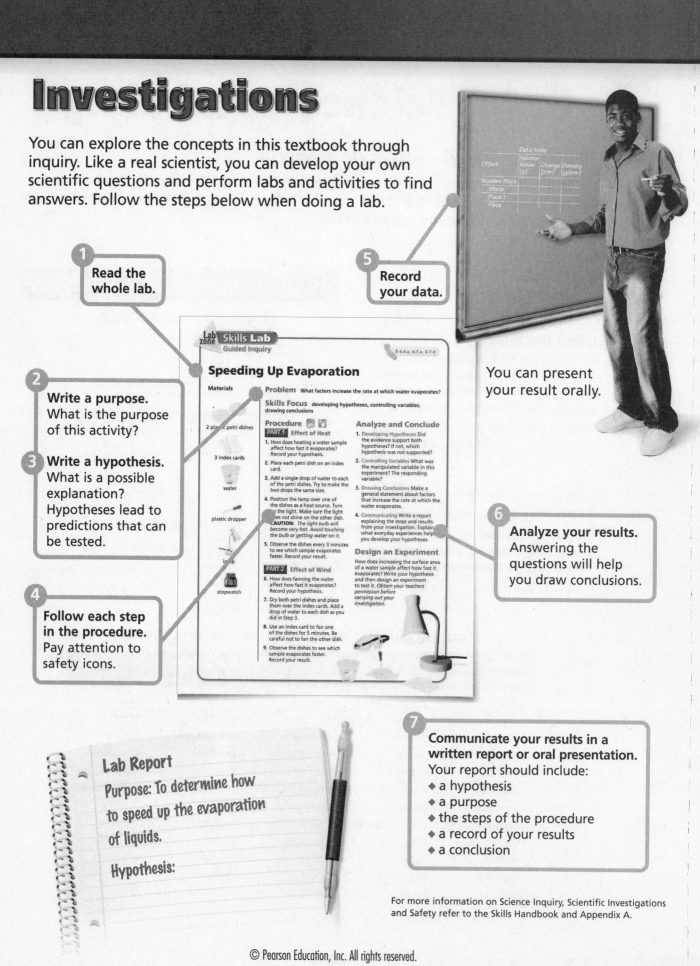

1 Read the whole lab.

5 Record your data.

You can present your result orally.

2 Write a purpose. What is the purpose of this activity?

3 Write a hypothesis. What is a possible explanation? Hypotheses lead to predictions that can be tested.

4 Follow each step in the procedure. Pay attention to safety icons.

6 Analyze your results. Answering the questions will help you draw conclusions.

Lab zone Skills Lab
Guided Inquiry
S 6.4.a, 6.7.a, 6.7.d

Speeding Up Evaporation

Materials
2 plastic petri dishes
3 index cards
water
plastic dropper
lamp
stopwatch

Problem What factors increase the rate at which water evaporates?

Skills Focus developing hypotheses, controlling variables, drawing conclusions

Procedure

PART 1 Effect of Heat
1. How does heating a water sample affect how fast it evaporates? Record your hypothesis.
2. Place each petri dish on an index card.
3. Add a single drop of water to each of the petri dishes. Try to make the two drops the same size.
4. Position the lamp over one of the dishes as a heat source. Turn on the light. Make sure the light does not shine on the other dish. **CAUTION:** *The light bulb will become very hot. Avoid touching the bulb or getting water on it.*
5. Observe the dishes every 3 minutes to see which sample evaporates faster. Record your result.

PART 2 Effect of Wind
6. How does fanning the water affect how fast it evaporates? Record your hypothesis.
7. Dry both petri dishes and place them over the index cards. Add a drop of water to each dish as you did in Step 3.
8. Use an index card to fan one of the dishes for 5 minutes. Be careful not to fan the other dish.
9. Observe the dishes to see which sample evaporates faster. Record your result.

Analyze and Conclude
1. Developing Hypotheses Did the evidence support both hypotheses? If not, which hypothesis was not supported?
2. Controlling Variables What was the manipulated variable in this experiment? The responding variable?
3. Drawing Conclusions Make a general statement about factors that increase the rate at which the water evaporates.
4. Communicating Write a report explaining the steps and results from your investigation. Explain what everyday experiences help you develop your hypotheses.

Design an Experiment
How does increasing the surface area of a water sample affect how fast it evaporates? Write your hypothesis and then design an experiment to test it. *Obtain your teachers permission before carrying out your investigation.*

Lab Report
Purpose: To determine how to speed up the evaporation of liquids.

Hypothesis:

7 Communicate your results in a written report or oral presentation. Your report should include:
- a hypothesis
- a purpose
- the steps of the procedure
- a record of your results
- a conclusion

For more information on Science Inquiry, Scientific Investigations and Safety refer to the Skills Handbook and Appendix A.

What Is Science?

Key Concepts

■ What skills do scientists use?

■ What is scientific inquiry?

■ How do scientific theories differ from scientific laws?

Science is a way of learning about the natural world. Science also includes all the knowledge gained from exploring the natural world. **As scientists seek to understand the natural world, they use skills such as observing, inferring, and predicting.**

Observing means using one or more of your senses to gather information. When you explain or interpret the things you observe, you are **inferring,** or making an inference. **Predicting** means making a forecast of what will happen in the future based on past experience or evidence.

Thinking and questioning are the start of the **scientific inquiry** process. **Scientific inquiry refers to the many ways in which scientists study the natural world and propose explanations based on the evidence they gather.** Scientific inquiry often begins with a problem or questions about an observation.

A **hypothesis** is a possible explanation for a set of observations or answer to a scientific question. In science, a hypothesis must be testable. This means that researchers must be able to carry out investigations and gather evidence that will either support or disprove the hypothesis.

A scientist designs an experiment to test a hypothesis. An experiment in which only one variable is manipulated at a time is called a **controlled experiment.** All factors that can change in an experiment are called **variables.** The variable that is purposely changed to test a hypothesis is called the **manipulated variable.** The factor that may change in response to the manipulated variable is called the **responding variable.**

A controlled experiment produces data. **Data** are facts, figures, and other evidence gathered through observations. After gathering and interpreting data, a scientist draws conclusions about the hypothesis. A scientist then communicates the results of the experiment through writing and speaking with other scientists.

A **scientific theory** is a well-tested explanation for a wide range of observations or experimental results. Future testing can prove a theory incorrect. A scientific law is a statement that describes what scientists expect to happen every time under a particular set of conditions. **Unlike a theory, a scientific law describes an observed pattern in nature, but does not provide an explanation for it.**

Introduction to Earth Science · *Reading/Notetaking Guide*

What Is Science? (pp. 6–12)

This section explains the skills that scientists use as they observe the natural world. The section also presents the process of scientific inquiry as a means of testing hypotheses and explains the difference between a scientific theory and a scientific law.

Use Target Reading Skills

Look at the illustration titled The Nature of Inquiry on page 11 of your textbook. In the graphic organizer below, ask three questions that you have about the illustration. As you read about scientific inquiry, write answers to your questions.

The Nature of Inquiry

Q. How does scientific inquiry begin?
A.
Q.
A.
Q.
A.

Thinking Like a Scientist (p. 7)

1. What is science?

    _____

    _____

    _____

Introduction to Earth Science · *Reading/Notetaking Guide*

2. What are three skills scientists use to learn more about the world?

_____

_____

3. What is observing?

_____

_____

_____

4. The senses a scientist uses in observing include sight, hearing, touch, taste, and

_____.

5. What is inferring?

_____

_____

_____

6. Circle the letter of each item that is true about inferences.
   a. Inferences are based on reasoning from what you already know.
   b. Making an inference involves guessing.
   c. An inference is an interpretation of observations.
   d. People make inferences all the time.

7. Making a forecast of what will happen in the future based on past experience or evidence is called _____.

Scientific Inquiry (pp. 8–11)

8. Write a sentence that explains what scientific inquiry is.

_____

_____

_____

_____

9. Is the following sentence true or false? Scientific inquiry often begins with drawing a conclusion. _____

Introduction to Earth Science · *Reading/Notetaking Guide*

What Is Science? *(continued)*

10. Circle the letter of each sentence that is a scientific question.

    a. At what temperature does water boil?
    b. When does the sun rise on April 3?
    c. How can my team work better together?
    d. Why does she like science more than he does?

11. A(n) _____ is a possible explanation for a set of observations.

12. Is the following sentence true or false? Scientists consider a hypothesis to be a fact. _____

13. To test a hypothesis, a scientist designs a(n) _____.

14. The facts, figures, and other evidence gathered through observations are called _____.

15. A(n) _____ is a decision about how to interpret what you have learned from an experiment.

    Complete the Nature of Inquiry diagram by filling in the blanks.

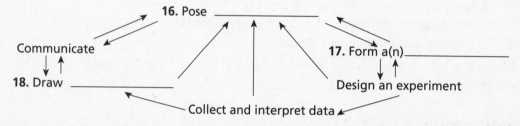

19. Why is scientific inquiry a process with many paths, not a rigid sequence of steps?

    _____

    _____

20. In scientific inquiry, what is communicating?

    _____

    _____

Scientific Theories and Laws (p. 12)

21. What is a scientific theory?

    _____

    _____

22. Is the following sentence true or false? Future testing can prove a scientific theory to be incorrect. _____

23. How is a scientific law unlike a scientific theory?

    _____

    _____

Chapter 1 Introduction to Earth Science • *Section 2 Summary*

Studying Earth

Key Concepts

- What are the parts of the Earth system?
- How is energy transferred in the Earth system?
- What are the branches of Earth science?

Energy is the ability to do work, or cause change. Energy from the sun is transferred to Earth as radiation, a form of energy that can move through space. Although the sun is millions of kilometers away, it affects everything on Earth's surface. The sun is part of a system that includes Earth's air, water, land, and living things. **The Earth system has four main parts, or "spheres": the atmosphere, hydrosphere, lithosphere, and biosphere. As one source of energy for processes on Earth, the sun can also be considered part of the Earth system.**

The outermost sphere is the **atmosphere,** the mixture of gases that surrounds the planet. Earth's oceans, lakes, rivers, and ice form the **hydrosphere.** Earth's solid, rocky outer layer is called the **lithosphere.** The lithosphere is made up of continents and islands, and it extends under the entire ocean floor. Energy from heat in Earth's interior drives some processes that shape the lithosphere. All living things—whether in the air, in the oceans, on land, or beneath the land surface—make up the **biosphere.**

Matter and energy constantly move from one part of the Earth system to another. **Matter** is what makes up everything in the universe. The movement of matter cannot occur without energy transfer. **Energy can be transferred from place to place by moving objects, by waves, or by heat flow.**

Any moving object or particle transfers energy. For example, wind and flowing water transfer energy through the movement of particles.

Energy can also be transferred by waves. A **wave** is an up-and-down or back-and-forth motion that carries energy from place to place but leaves the matter behind. Sound waves, water waves, and earthquake waves are types of waves that require a medium to travel through. A medium is a material through which a wave travels. Another type of wave, the electromagnetic wave, does not require a medium to travel through. Electromagnetic waves transfer electrical and magnetic energy.

Heat is the energy transferred from one object to another as a result of a difference in temperature. **Thermal energy** is the total energy of all the atoms that make up an object. Heat flow occurs when two objects at different temperatures are brought into contact. Heat always flows from the warmer object to the cooler object.

Earth science is the body of knowledge about Earth's land, air, water, and living things. **Earth science has several different branches. In this book, you will learn about geology, meteorology, and environmental science.** Geology is the study of the solid Earth. Meteorology is the study of Earth's atmosphere. Environmental scientists study Earth's environment and resources.

Introduction to Earth Science • *Reading/Notetaking Guide*

Studying Earth (pp. 13–19)

This section describes the four main parts of the Earth system. The section also describes energy transfer within the Earth system and several branches of Earth science.

Use Target Reading Skills

Preview the red heading The Structure of the Earth System *and the blue subheadings* Earth as a System, Atmosphere, Hydrosphere, Lithosphere, Biosphere. *Complete the graphic organizer below by answering the question that is asked about each heading.*

The Structure of the Earth System

Heading	Question	Answer
Earth as a System, Atmosphere	What is a system?	A system is a group of parts that work together as a whole.
Atmosphere	What is the atmosphere?	a.
Hydrosphere	What is the hydrosphere?	b.
Lithosphere	What is the lithosphere?	c.
Biosphere	What is the biosphere, and how does it relate to Earth's other spheres?	d.

The Structure of the Earth System (pp. 14–15)

1. The ability to do work or cause change is known as

   _____.

2. Is the following sentence true or false? The sun can be considered part of the Earth system. _____

Introduction to Earth Science ▪ *Reading/Notetaking Guide*

Match each sphere of the Earth system with its description.

Sphere	Description
____ 3. lithosphere	**a.** solid, rocky layer
____ 4. biosphere	**b.** a mixture of gases
____ 5. atmosphere	**c.** oceans, lakes, rivers, and ice
____ 6. hydrosphere	**d.** all living things

Energy Transfer: A Big Idea (pp. 16–17)

7. Is the following sentence true or false? The movement of matter cannot occur without energy transfer. _____

8. List three ways by which energy can be transferred from place to place.

   _____

   _____

   _____

9. Describe what a wave is.

   _____

   _____

   _____

10. Is the following sentence true or false? Waves transfer matter and energy from place to place. _____

11. Is the following sentence true or false? All waves need a medium to travel through. _____

12. The transfer of thermal energy from one object to another due to a difference in temperature is known as _____.

13. Describe the direction of heat flow when a warm object and a cool object touch.

   _____

   _____

   _____

Introduction to Earth Science · *Reading/Notetaking Guide*

Studying Earth *(continued)*

The Branches of Earth Science (pp. 18–19)

Match each branch of Earth science with its area of study.

Branch of Earth Science	Area of Study
____ 14. geology	a. Earth's environment and resources
____ 15. meteorology	b. Earth's atmosphere
____ 16. environmental science	c. solid Earth

Chapter 1 Introduction to Earth Science • *Section 3 Summary*

Exploring Earth's Surface

Key Concepts

■ What does the topography of an area include?

■ What are the main types of landforms?

■ How do maps represent Earth's surface and help find locations?

Topography is the shape of the land. An area's topography may be flat, sloping, hilly, or mountainous. **The topography of an area includes the area's elevation, relief, and landforms.** The height above sea level of a point on Earth's surface is its **elevation.** The difference between the highest and the lowest points of an area is its **relief.**

A landform is a feature of topography formed by the processes that shape Earth's surface. Different landforms have different combinations of elevation and relief.

There are three main types of landforms: plains, mountains, and plateaus. A **plain** is a landform made up of flat or gently rolling land with low relief. A plain that lies along a seacoast is called a costal plain. In North America, a coastal plain extends around the continent's eastern and southeastern shores. Coastal plains have both low elevation and low relief. A plain that lies away from the coast is called an interior plain. Although interior plains have low relief, their elevation can vary. The broad interior plains of North America are called the Great Plains.

A **mountain** is a landform with high elevation and high relief. Mountains usually occur as part of a mountain range. A mountain range is a group of mountains that are closely related in shape, structure, or age. The different mountain ranges in a region make up a mountain system. Mountain ranges and mountain systems in a long, connected chain form a larger unit called a mountain belt. The Rocky Mountains are part of a mountain belt that stretches down the sides of North and South America.

A landform that has high elevation and a more or less level surface is called a **plateau.** A plateau is rarely perfectly smooth on top. Streams and rivers may cut into the plateau's surface.

A **map** is a flat model of all or part of Earth's surface as seen from above. A map's **scale** relates distances on a map to distances on Earth's surface. **Maps are drawn to scale and use symbols to represent topography and other features on Earth's surface.**

Two lines, the equator and the prime meridian, are the baselines for measuring distances on Earth. Using these lines, mapmakers have constructed a grid made up of lines of latitude and longitude. **Degrees** can be used to measure distances on the surface of a sphere. **The lines of latitude and longitude on a map form a grid that can be used to find locations anywhere on Earth.** The distance in degrees north or south of the equator is called **latitude.** The distance in degrees east or west of the prime meridian is called **longitude.**

Introduction to Earth Science • *Reading/Notetaking Guide*

Exploring Earth's Surface (pp. 21–27)

This section describes factors that determine the shape of Earth's land surface. The section also describes how scientists divide Earth into four spheres.

Use Target Reading Skills

As you read, complete the compare/contrast table to show the similarities and differences among the types of landforms.

Characteristics of Landforms

Landform	Elevation	Relief
Plain	a. _____	Low
Mountain	b. _____	c. _____
d. _____	High	e. _____

Introduction (p. 21)

1. The shape of the land is referred to as _____.

Match the term with its definition.

Term	Definition
____ 2. elevation	a. Difference in elevation
____ 3. relief	b. Height above sea level
____ 4. landform	c. Feature of topography

Match the type of landform with its characteristics.

Landform	Characteristics
____ 5. plain	a. High elevation and high relief
____ 6. mountain	b. High elevation and level surface
____ 7. plateau	c. Flat land and low relief

Name _____ Date _____ Class _____

Introduction to Earth Science ▪ *Reading/Notetaking Guide*

Types of Landforms (pp. 22–23)

8. Complete the concept map.

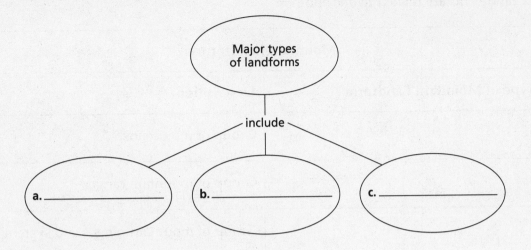

9. A plain that lies along a seacoast is called a(n)
   _____.

10. A plain that lies away from the coast is called a(n) _____.

11. Is the following sentence true or false? Interior plains may have high
    relief. _____

12. How is a plateau similar to a plain?
    _____
    _____

Introduction to Earth Science · *Reading/Notetaking Guide*

Exploring Earth's Surface *(continued)*

13. Complete the table to show how the different types of mountain landforms are related to one another.

Mountain Landforms	
Type of Mountain Landform	**Description**
a.	Group of mountains
b.	Group of mountain ranges
c.	Group of mountain ranges and systems

    d. Explain how the types of mountain landforms are related to one another.

_____

_____

_____

_____

14. The Cascade Range in Washington, Oregon, and California is a
_____.

15. The Santa Lucia Mountains are one mountain range in a
_____ known as the Coast Ranges.

16. Mountain ranges and mountain systems form a larger unit called a
_____.

17. The _____ in Washington State is an example of a plateau.

Introduction to Earth Science · *Reading/Notetaking Guide*

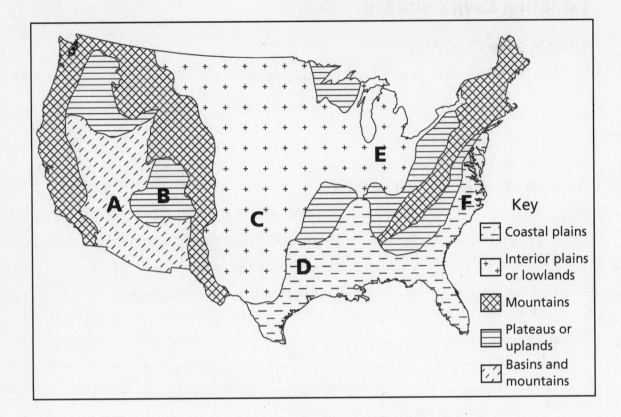

18. What type of landforms would you expect to find in Region A? Region B?

_____

_____

_____

_____

19. Which landform region would you expect to have a higher elevation, C or D? Explain.

_____

_____

20. If you traveled in a straight line from Region E to Region F, how would the topography change?

_____

_____

Introduction to Earth Science · *Reading/Notetaking Guide*

Exploring Earth's Surface (continued)

What Is a Map? (p. 24)

21. A flat model of all or part of Earth's surface is a(n) _____.

22. Maps are drawn _____ and use symbols to represent Earth's features.

Match the map feature with the role it plays.

Map Feature	**Role It Plays**
____ 23. scale	a. Stands for a feature on Earth's surface
____ 24. symbol	b. Relates distance on a map to distance on Earth's surface
____ 25. key	c. Lists and explains all the symbols on a map

26. What are some of the physical and human-made features that map symbols can represent?

_____

_____

_____

27. What does a map scale of 1:25,000 mean?

_____

_____

_____

Earth's Grid (pp. 25–27)

28. The units scientists use to measure distances around a circle are _____.

29. The imaginary line that circles Earth halfway between the North and South poles is the _____.

30. Half of Earth's surface is called a(n) _____.

31. Circle the letter of each sentence that is true about the prime meridian.

   a. It makes a half circle from the North Pole to the South Pole.
   b. It passes through Washington, D.C.
   c. It divides Earth into the Northern and Southern Hemispheres.
   d. It passes through the Northern and Southern Hemispheres.

Introduction to Earth Science ▪ *Reading/Notetaking Guide*

32. Circle the letter of each sentence that is true about latitude.

    a. The prime meridian is the starting line for measuring latitude.

    b. Latitude measures distance in degrees north or south of the equator.

    c. All lines of latitude are parallel to the equator.

    d. The latitude of the North Pole is 90° north.

33. Circle the letter of each sentence that is true about longitude.

    a. The equator is the starting line for measuring longitude.

    b. Longitude measures distance in degrees east or west of the prime meridian.

    c. All lines of longitude meet at the equator.

    d. Lines of longitude cross lines of latitude at 45° angles.

34. Label the lines on the map with the following terms: equator, prime meridian, 30°N latitude, 30°W longitude.

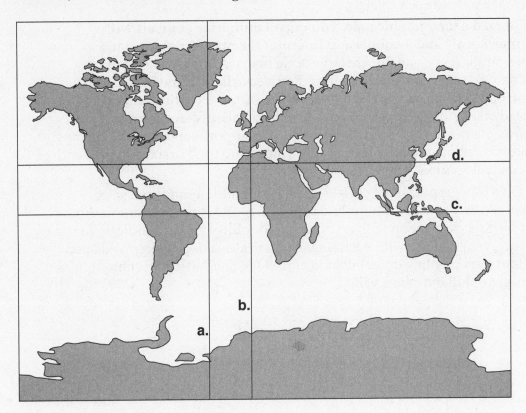

35. What is the longitude of the prime meridian?

_____

_____

Topographic Maps

Key Concepts

- How do mapmakers represent elevation, relief, and slope?

- How do you read a topographic map?

A **topographic map** provides information on the elevation, relief, and slope of the ground surface. **Mapmakers use contour lines to represent elevation, relief, and slope on topographic maps.** On topographic maps, a **contour line** connects points of equal elevation. The change in elevation from contour line to contour line is called the **contour interval.** The contour interval for a given map is always the same. Usually, every fifth contour line, known as an index contour, is darker and heavier than the others. **Index contours** are labeled with the elevation above sea level in round units, such as 2,000 feet above sea level.

   To read a topographic map, you must familiarize yourself with the map's scale and symbols and interpret the map's contour lines. Topographic maps usually are large-scale maps. A large-scale map is one that shows a close-up view of part of Earth's surface. In the United States, most topographic maps are at a scale of 1:24,000, or 1 centimeter equals 0.24 kilometers. At this scale, a map can show the details of elevation and features such as rivers and coastlines. Large buildings, airports, and major highways appear as outlines at the correct scale. Symbols are used to show houses and other small features.

   On a topographic map, closely spaced contour lines indicate steep slopes. Widely spaced contour lines indicate gentle slopes. A contour line that forms a closed loop with no other contour lines inside it indicates a hilltop. A closed loop with dashes inside indicates a depression. V-shaped contour lines pointing downhill indicate a ridge line. V-shaped contour lines pointing uphill indicate a valley.

Introduction to Earth Science • *Reading/Notetaking Guide*

Topographic Maps (pp. 28–31)

This section describes a special type of map called a topographic map. It also describes how and why topographic maps are used.

Use Target Reading Skills

Review the red heading Reading a Topographic Map *and the blue subheadings* Scale, Symbols, *and* Interpreting Contour Lines. *Complete the graphic organizer below by answering the question that is asked about each heading.*

Topographic Maps

Heading	Question	Answer
Reading a Topographic Map	What must I know in order to read a topographic map?	You must familiarize yourself with the map's scale and symbols and be able to interpret contour lines.
Scale	What scale is commonly used on topographic maps?	**a.**
Symbols	What symbols are used on a topographic map?	**b.**
Interpreting Contour Lines	What does the spacing between contour lines tell you?	**c.**

Mapping Earth's Topography (p. 29)

1. A map that provides information on the elevation, relief, and slope of the ground surface is called a(n) _____ map.

2. List three types of information about the ground surface that are provided by topographic maps.

   a. _____   b. _____

   c. _____

3. Every fifth contour line, or _____, is usually darker and heavier than the other contour lines.

4. Is the following sentence true or false? The contour interval for a given topographic map is always the same. _____

Introduction to Earth Science • *Reading/Notetaking Guide*

Topographic Maps *(continued)*

Reading a Topographic Map *(pp. 30–31)*

5. Is the following sentence true or false? Every other contour line on a topographic map is labeled with the elevation. _____

6. Circle the number of contour lines you would need to show a change in elevation of 1,000 feet on a map with a contour interval of 200 feet.

   a. 5   **b.** 10
   c. 20   **d.** 50

7. Circle the contour interval if ten contour lines show a change in elevation of 2,000 feet.

   a. 10 feet   **b.** 100 feet
   c. 200 feet   **d.** 500 feet

8. Complete the table with the definition of each type of contour symbol.

Type of Symbol	Definition
Contour Line	a.
Contour Interval	b.
Index Contour	c.

   d. Suppose two cities in the United States have the same elevation. Which type of contour symbol would connect them? _____

   e. Suppose you are looking at a contour symbol labeled "2500." Which type of symbol is it? _____

9. How close the contour lines are is an indication of an area's _____.

Introduction to Earth Science ▪ *Reading/Notetaking Guide*

10. What do V-shaped contour lines indicate when they point downhill?
    When they point uphill?

    _____

    _____

    _____

    _____

11. Label each section of topographic map to indicate whether it shows a
    steep slope, a gentle slope, a depression, or a hilltop.

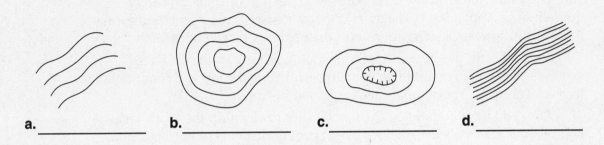

a._____   b._____   c._____   d._____

Safety in the Science Laboratory

Key Concepts

- Why is preparation important when carrying out scientific investigations in the lab and in the field?

- What should you do if an accident occurs?

Good preparation helps you stay safe when doing science activities in the laboratory. Preparing for a lab should begin the day before you will perform the lab. It is important to read through the procedure carefully and make sure you understand all the directions. Also, review the general safety guidelines in Appendix A. The most important safety rule is simple: Always follow your teacher's instructions and the textbook directions exactly.

Labs and activities in your textbook include safety symbols. These symbols alert you to possible dangers in performing the lab and remind you to work carefully. The symbols are explained in Appendix A.

When you have completed the lab, be sure to clean up the work area. Follow your teacher's instructions about proper disposal of wastes. Finally, be sure to wash your hands thoroughly after working in the laboratory.

Some investigations will be done in the "field." The field can be any outdoor area, such as a schoolyard, a forest, a park, or a beach. **Just as in the laboratory, good preparation helps you stay safe when doing science activities in the field.** There can be many potential safety hazards outdoors, including severe weather, traffic, wild animals, or poisonous plants. Advance planning may help you avoid some potential hazards. Whenever you do field work, always tell an adult where you will be. Never carry out a field investigation alone.

At some point, an accident can occur in the lab. **When any accident occurs, no matter how minor, notify your teacher immediately. Then, listen to your teacher's directions and carry them out quickly.** Make sure you know the location and proper use of all the emergency equipment in your lab room. Knowing safety and first-aid procedures beforehand will prepare you to handle accidents properly.

Introduction to Earth Science • *Reading/Notetaking Guide*

Safety in the Science Laboratory (pp. 33–37)

This section explains why preparation is important when carrying out scientific investigations. It also describes what you should do if an accident occurs.

Use Target Reading Skills

As you read, make an outline about science safety that you can use for review. Use the red headings for the main ideas and the blue headings for supporting ideas.

Safety in the Science Laboratory

I. Safety in the Lab

    A. Preparing for the Lab

    B.

    C.

II. Safety in the Field

III. In Case of an Accident

Safety in the Lab (pp. 34–36)

1. Is the following sentence true or false? No amount of preparation can help you with safety when doing science activities in the laboratory. _____

2. Circle the letter that states when you should begin preparing for a lab.
   a. 1 hour ahead of the lab
   b. 10 minutes ahead of the lab
   c. the morning of the lab
   d. 1 day before doing the lab

3. In preparing for a lab, it is important to review the general safety guidelines, which can be found in _____ of your textbook.

4. What should you do if something is unclear to you about the lab before you begin?
   _____
   _____

5. What is the most important safety rule when performing a lab?
   _____
   _____

6. Is the following sentence true or false? You should never try anything on your own in the lab without asking your teacher first. _____

Introduction to Earth Science · *Reading/Notetaking Guide*

Safety in the Science Laboratory *(continued)*

7. Circle the letter of each sentence that is true about safety symbols.

   a. They identify safety equipment that you should use.

   b. They alert you to possible dangers in doing the lab.

   c. They give you specific instructions about each lab in the book.

   d. They remind you to work carefully.

Match the symbol with its meaning by writing the correct letter beside each symbol.

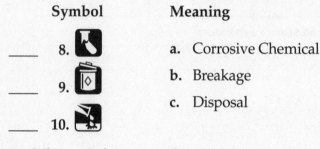

Symbol	Meaning
____ 8.	**a.** Corrosive Chemical
____ 9.	**b.** Breakage
____ 10.	**c.** Disposal

11. When you have completed a lab, you should _____ your work area.

12. How should lab wastes be disposed of?

    _____

    _____

13. Is the following sentence true or false? You should wash your hands after working in the laboratory even if you don't think they're dirty. _____

Safety in the Field *(p. 36)*

14. Circle the letter of each step you should take whenever you do field work.

   a. Work alone as much as possible.

   b. Dress appropriately for any conditions you will encounter.

   c. Tell an adult where you will be.

   d. Ask an adult or classmate to accompany you.

15. Possible hazards that you might encounter during a field investigation include

   a. traffic.   **b.** severe weather.

   c. poisonous plants.   **d.** all of the above.

In Case of an Accident *(p. 37)*

16. What should you do immediately whenever an accident occurs?

    _____

17. Circle the letter of each step you should take if you spill something on your skin while doing a lab.

   a. Cover the skin with a clean dressing.

   b. Wash your hands.

   c. Flush the skin with large amounts of water.

   d. Do nothing unless the skin blisters.

Minerals and Rocks

Key Concepts

- What is a mineral?
- What are the three major groups of rock, and how do they form through the rock cycle?
- How are minerals and rocks used and processed?

A mineral is a naturally occurring, inorganic solid that forms on or beneath Earth's surface. Almost all minerals have a crystal shape. Each mineral has a definite chemical composition. More than 3,000 minerals have been identified.

Rocks are made up of a combination of minerals. **Geologists classify rocks into three major groups: igneous rock, sedimentary rock, and metamorphic rock. The rocks in each group form through different steps in the rock cycle.**

Igneous rocks form from molten material deep inside Earth. The material slowly cools and hardens to form a rock. If the material cools slowly, large crystals form. If the material cools quickly, small crystals form.

Sedimentary rocks are made from pieces of rocks that have been broken down by processes involving water and weather. The pieces are called sediment. **Sediment** can also contain remains of plants and animals. The sediment gets moved by water and wind and gets deposited in layers. Over millions of years, the sediments are squeezed together and become sedimentary rock.

Metamorphic rocks form when rocks are exposed to a great increase in temperature and pressure. This occurs deep within Earth's interior where it is hotter and the overlying rock cause great pressure. Minerals may get changed to other minerals forming a new rock. Mineral grains also become aligned in response to the increased pressure. If the heat and pressure become too great, the rock melts and the rock cycle begins again.

Minerals are the source of gemstones, metals, and other materials used to make many products. Gemstones are hard, colorful minerals that are used not only for jewelry but also for cutting, grinding and polishing. Minerals are used in foods, medicine, fertilizer, and building materials. Minerals are also the source of metals such as copper, iron, and silver.

Today, people use rocks for building materials and in industrial processes. A rock that contains a metal or mineral that can be mined and sold for a profit is called an **ore. To produce metal from ore, the ore must be mined, or removed from the ground. Then the ore must be processed to extract the metal.** Mining is done in one of three ways. Strip mining removes the overlying layers of soil and rock to reveal the ore beneath. Open pit mining involves digging a huge pit to get to the ore. Shaft mining is used when the ore occurs in veins far beneath the surface.

The mined ore must be processed before it can be used. During **smelting,** the ore is mixed with other substances and then melted. The useful ore separates from the rest of the rock. The pure ore is removed.

Weathering and Soil • *Reading/Notetaking Guide*

Minerals and Rocks (pp. 48–55)

This section describes what minerals are. It also describes how minerals combine to form rocks and how rocks form.

Use Target Reading Skills

Look at the illustration titled How Sedimentary Rocks Form *on page 51 of your textbook. In the graphic organizer below, ask three questions that you have about the illustration. As you read about sedimentary rocks, write answers to your questions.*

How Sedimentary Rocks Form

Q. What are sedimentary rocks made of?
A.
Q.
A.
Q.
A.

What Is a Mineral? (p. 49)

1. Complete the chart to describe the characteristics of a mineral.

A mineral must have/be:
a. definite chemical composition
b.
c.
d.
e.

Weathering and Soil • *Reading/Notetaking Guide*

2. Is the following sentence true or false? Diamonds that are created in the laboratory are considered minerals. _____

Rocks and the Rock Cycle (pp. 50–52)

3. List the three main types of rocks.

   _____

   _____

   _____

4. Is the following sentence true or false? Igneous rocks form only beneath Earth's surface. _____

Match the rock's speed of cooling with the characteristics of its crystals.

Cooling Speed

_____ 5. cooled slowly

_____ 6. cooled quickly

Crystal Characteristic

a. large, well-formed crystals

b. small, barely visible crystals

7. What is sediment?

   _____

   _____

   _____

8. Complete the flowchart to describe how sedimentary rocks are formed.

Sediment is deposited in layers.	a.	Sediments get b.

Minerals in the rock slowly dissolve in water.	c.	Sediments change to sedimentary rock.

9. Circle the letter of each sentence that is true about sedimentary rocks.

   a. Sedimentary rocks contain particles from other rocks.
   b. Sedimentary rocks may contain shells and skeletons of marine animals such as coral.
   c. Sedimentary rocks are crystals that form as water evaporates.
   d. Sedimentary rocks are crystals that form as magma cools.

Weathering and Soil • *Reading/Notetaking Guide*

Minerals and Rocks *(continued)*

10. What two factors cause rocks to become metamorphic rocks?

    a. _____

    b. _____

11. What happens to the minerals when a rock becomes a metamorphic rock?

    _____

    _____

Using Minerals and Rocks (p. 53)

12. What are some uses for minerals?

    a. _____

    b. _____

    c. _____

13. Circle the letter of each choice that is a possible use of rocks.

    a. floors and kitchen counters
    b. walls of buildings
    c. roofing
    d. cement and steel

Producing Metals From Ores (pp. 54–55)

14. What is an ore?

    _____

    _____

15. Which type of mining would be used to extract a vein of ore from deep underground?

    a. strip mining
    b. open-pit mining
    c. shaft mining
    d. offshore mining

16. How is land restored after mining is completed?

    _____

    _____

    _____

17. The process that turns ore into useful metals is called

    _____.

Chapter 2 Weathering and Soil • *Section 2 Summary*

Rocks and Weathering

Key Concepts

- How do weathering and erosion affect Earth's surface?

- What are the causes of mechanical weathering and chemical weathering?

- What determines how fast weathering occurs?

Weathering is the process that breaks down rock and other substances of Earth's surface. **Erosion** is the removal of rock particles by wind, water, ice, or gravity. **Topography is reshaped by weathering and erosion. These processes work together continuously to wear down and carry away the rocks at Earth's surface.** The weathering and erosion that geologists observe today also shaped Earth's surface millions of years ago. How do geologists know this? Geologists make inferences based on the principle of **uniformitarianism.** This principle states that the same processes that operate today operated in the past.

There are two kinds of weathering: mechanical weathering and chemical weathering. Both types of weathering act slowly, but over time they break down even the biggest, hardest rocks. The type of weathering in which rock is physically broken into smaller pieces is called **mechanical weathering. The causes of mechanical weathering include freezing and thawing, release of pressure, plant growth, actions of animals, and abrasion.** The term **abrasion** refers to the grinding away of rock by rock particles carried by water, ice, wind, or gravity.

In cool climates, water expands when it freezes and acts as a wedge. This process is called **ice wedging.** With repeated freezing and thawing, cracks slowly expand until pieces of rock break off.

Another type of weathering that attacks rocks is **chemical weathering,** a process that breaks down rock through chemical changes. **The causes of chemical weathering include the action of water, oxygen, carbon dioxide, living organisms, and acid rain.** Chemical weathering can produce new minerals as it breaks down rock. Chemical and mechanical weathering often work together. As mechanical weathering breaks rocks into pieces, more surface area becomes exposed to chemical weathering.

Water is the most important cause of chemical weathering. Water weathers rock by dissolving it. The oxygen in air is an important cause of chemical weathering. Iron combines with oxygen in the presence of water in a process called **oxidation.** The product of oxidation is rust.

The most important factors that determine the rate at which weathering occurs are the type of rock and the climate. Some types of rock weather more rapidly than others. For example, some rock weathers easily because it is **permeable,** which means that it is full of air spaces that allow water to seep through it.

Weathering and Soil · *Reading/Notetaking Guide*

Rocks and Weathering (pp. 56–63)

This section describes how rocks are broken down by forces of weathering. The section also describes factors that determine how quickly weathering occurs.

Use Target Reading Skills

As you read about mechanical weathering, complete the graphic organizer by filling in the details.

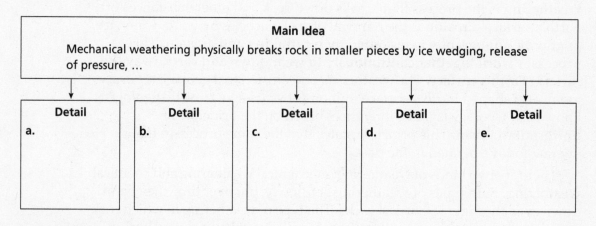

Main Idea

Mechanical weathering physically breaks rock in smaller pieces by ice wedging, release of pressure, ...

Detail	Detail	Detail	Detail	Detail
a.	b.	c.	d.	e.

Weathering and Erosion (p. 57)

Match the process with its description.

Process

____ **1.** weathering

____ **2.** erosion

Description

a. Movement of rock particles by wind, water, ice, or gravity

b. Breaking down of rock and other substances at Earth's surface

3. Complete the concept map.

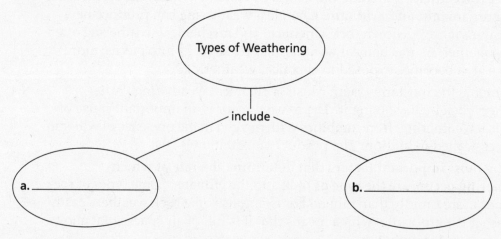

Types of Weathering

include

a. _____

b. _____

Mechanical Weathering (pp. 58–59)

4. The type of weathering in which rock is physically broken into smaller pieces is called _____ weathering.

5. List the types of mechanical weathering.

   a. _____ b. _____

   c. _____ d. _____

   e. _____

6. What is abrasion?

   _____

   _____

   _____

7. Complete the cycle diagram.

Ice Wedging

Water seeps into cracks.

a. _____

Ice widens cracks.

b. _____

Weathering and Soil · *Reading/Notetaking Guide*

Rocks and Weathering *(continued)*

8. Would ice-wedging be an important cause of mechanical weathering near Earth's equator? Explain.

   _____

   _____

Chemical Weathering (pp. 60–61)

9. The process that breaks down rock through chemical changes is _____ weathering.

10. List the agents of chemical weathering.

    a. _____ b. _____

    c. _____ d. _____

    e. _____

11. Is the following sentence true or false? Chemical weathering produces rock particles with the same mineral makeup as the rock they came from.

    _____

Match the cause of chemical weathering with the statement that is true about it.

Cause	**Statement**
_____ 12. water	a. It causes iron to rust.
_____ 13. oxygen	b. It is caused by pollution.
_____ 14. carbon dioxide	c. It is the most important cause.
_____ 15. living organisms	d. It forms carbonic acid.
_____ 16. acid rain	e. Lichens are one example.

17. Is the following sentence true or false? Water weathers rock by gradually dissolving it.

    _____

18. Oxygen weathers rock through a process called _____.

19. List two kinds of rock that are easily weathered by carbonic acid.

    a. _____ b. _____

Weathering and Soil • *Reading/Notetaking Guide*

20. How do plants dissolve rock?

_____

_____

_____

Rate of Weathering (pp. 62–63)

21. The most important factors that determine the rate of weathering are
type of rock and _____.

22. Is the following sentence true or false? The minerals that make up a rock
determine how fast it weathers.

_____

23. A rock that is full of tiny, connected air spaces is said to be

_____.

24. Why does a permeable rock weather chemically at a fast rate?

_____

_____

_____

25. Why does chemical weathering occur more quickly in a hot climate?

_____

_____

_____

How Soil Forms

Key Concepts

- What is soil made of, and how does it form?
- How do scientists classify soils?
- What is the role of plants and animals in soil formation?

Soil is the loose, weathered material on Earth's surface in which plants can grow. **Bedrock** is the solid layer of rock beneath the soil.

Soil is a mixture of rock particles, minerals, decayed organic material, air, and water. The decayed organic material in soil is **humus,** a dark-colored substance that forms as plant and animal remains decay. Humus helps create spaces in soil for air and water that plants must have. The **fertility** of soil is a measure of how well the soil supports plant growth.

Soil texture depends on the size of individual particles. The largest soil particles are gravel. Next in size are sand particles, followed by silt particles. Clay particles are the smallest. Texture is important for plant growth. Plants can "drown" for lack of air in clay soil, and they may die from lack of water in sandy soil. The best soil for growing most plants is **loam,** which is soil that is made up of about equal parts of clay, sand, and silt.

Soil forms as rock is broken down by weathering and mixes with other materials on the surface. It is constantly formed wherever bedrock is exposed. Soil formation continues over a long period, and gradually soil develops layers called horizons. A **soil horizon** is a layer of soil that differs in color and texture from the layers above or below it. The top layer, the A horizon, is made up of **topsoil,** a crumbly, dark brown soil that is a mixture of humus, clay, and other minerals. The next layer, the B horizon, often called **subsoil,** usually consists of clay and other particles washed down from the A horizon, but little humus. Below that layer is the C horizon, which contains only partly weathered rock.

Scientists classify different types of soil into major groups based on climate, plants, and soil composition. The most common plants found in a region are also used to help classify the soil. Soils are classified as either **acidic** or **basic.** The most fertile soils have a pH between 6 and 7.5.

Soil teems with living things. **Some soil organisms make humus, the material that makes soil fertile. Other soil organisms mix the soil and make spaces in it for air and water.** Plants contribute most of the organic remains that form humus. The leaves that plants shed form a loose layer on the ground called **litter.** Humus forms in a process called decomposition, in which organisms that live in the soil turn dead organic material into humus. The organisms that break the remains of dead organisms into smaller pieces and digest them with chemicals are called **decomposers.** Fungi, bacteria, worms, and other organisms are the main soil decomposers. Earthworms do most of the work of mixing humus with other materials in soil. Earthworms and burrowing animals also help aerate, or mix air into, the soil.

Weathering and Soil • *Reading/Notetaking Guide*

How Soil Forms (pp. 66–72)

This section explains how soil forms. The section also describes several features of soil, such as soil horizons and the living things found in soil.

Use Target Reading Skills

Look at the illustration titled Soil Layers *on page 68 of your textbook. In the graphic organizer below, ask three questions that you have about the illustration. As you read about how soil forms, write answers to your questions.*

Soil Layers

Q. What is the first step in the formation of soil?
A.
Q. What are soil horizons?
A.
Q. How do the A horizon and B horizon form?
A.

43

Weathering and Soil · *Reading/Notetaking Guide*

How Soil Forms *(continued)*

What Is Soil? (pp. 66–67)

1. The loose, weathered material on Earth's surface in which plants can grow is _____.

2. The solid layer of rock beneath the soil is called _____.

3. What is soil composed of?

   _____

   _____

   _____

4. List the three types of weathered rock particles found in soil.

   a. _____   b. _____

   c. _____

5. The decayed organic material in soil is called _____.

6. Circle the letter of the choice that lists soil particles from largest to smallest.

   a. sand, gravel, clay, silt
   b. gravel, sand, silt, clay
   c. gravel, silt, sand, clay
   d. gravel, sand, clay, silt

7. Soil that is made up of about equal parts of clay, sand, and silt is called _____.

The Process of Soil Formation (p. 68)

8. How does soil form?

   _____

   _____

   _____

Weathering and Soil · *Reading/Notetaking Guide*

Match the soil horizon with its makeup.

Soil Horizon	Makeup
____ 9. A	a. Topsoil
____ 10. B	b. Weathered rock particles
____ 11. C	c. Subsoil

12. Label each of the soil horizons shown in the three drawings as A, B, or C horizon.

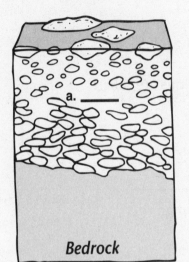
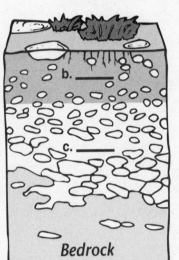
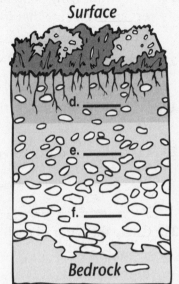

13. Circle the letter of each sentence that is true about the rate of soil formation.

    a. It is faster in areas that are cold.

    b. It is slower in areas that are dry.

    c. It is faster with limestone than granite.

    d. It is unaffected by the type of rock being weathered.

Soil Types (p. 69)

14. Circle the letter of each factor that scientists use to classify the different types of soil into groups.

    a. climate

    b. plant types

    c. soil composition

    d. size of animal populations

15. Is the following sentence true or false? Plants grow well in soil that is either strongly acidic or strongly basic.

_____

Weathering and Soil · *Reading/Notetaking Guide*

How Soil Forms *(continued)*

Living Organisms in Soil (pp. 70–72)

16. How do soil organisms improve soil?

_____

_____

_____

17. Is the following sentence true or false? Animals contribute most of the organic remains that form humus.

_____

18. As plants shed leaves, they form a loose layer called

_____.

19. Soil organisms that turn dead organic matter into humus are called

_____.

20. List four soil decomposers.

a. _____   b. _____

c. _____   d. _____

21. Circle the letter of each choice that is an example of fungi.

   a. molds

   b. mushrooms

   c. bacteria

   d. earthworms

22. Is the following sentence true or false? Earthworms do most of the work of mixing humus with other materials in soil.

_____

23. How can burrowing mammals improve soil?

_____

_____

_____

Chapter 2 Weathering and Soil • *Section 4 Summary*

Soil Conservation

Key Concepts

- Why is fertile soil considered a nonrenewable resource?

- How can soil lose its value?

- What are some ways that soil can be conserved?

The prairie soils of the central United States took many thousands of years to develop. Prairie soil was once rich with humus because it was covered with tall grass. The **sod**—the thick mass of tough roots at the surface of the soil—kept the soil in place and held onto moisture. Today, farm crops have replaced the prairies. But prairie soils are still among the richest in the world.

A **natural resource** is anything in the environment that humans use. Soil is one of Earth's most valuable resources because everything that lives on land, including humans, depends directly or indirectly on soil. Plants depend directly on soil to live and grow. Animals depend on plants for food. Fertile soil is valuable because there is a limited supply. It can take hundreds of years for just a few centimeters of soil to develop. **Because fertile soil is in limited supply and takes a long time to form, it is considered a nonrenewable resource.**

The value of soil is reduced when soil loses its fertility and when topsoil is lost due to erosion. This occurred in large parts of the South in the late 1800s in areas where only cotton had been grown. In the early 1900s, a scientist named George Washington Carver developed new crops and farming methods that helped restore soil fertility in the South.

Soil can be lost to erosion by water or wind. Water or wind erosion can occur wherever soil is not protected by plant cover. Plants break the force of rain, and plant roots hold soil in place.

Wind erosion was the cause of soil loss on the Great Plains in the 1930s. By 1930, almost all of the Great Plains had been turned into farms or ranches. Plowing removed the grass from the Great Plains and exposed the soil. In times of drought, the topsoil quickly dried out, turned to dust, and blew away. Wind blew the soil east in great, black clouds. The problem was most serious in the southern Plains states. This area was called the **Dust Bowl.** The Dust Bowl helped people appreciate the value of soil.

Soil conservation is the management of soil to prevent its destruction. **Soil can be conserved through contour plowing, conservation plowing, and crop rotation. Contour plowing** is the practice of plowing fields along the curves of a slope. This prevents rain from washing soil away. **Conservation plowing** disturbs the soil and its plant cover as little as possible. Dead weeds and stalks of the previous year's crop are left in the ground to help return soil nutrients, retain moisture, and hold soil in place. In **crop rotation,** every year different crops are planted in the field.

Weathering and Soil · *Reading/Notetaking Guide*

Soil Conservation (pp. 74–77)

This section explains why soil is valuable. The section also explains how soil can be damaged or lost, as well as how it can be conserved.

Use Target Reading Skills

Look at the map and photo of the Dust Bowl in your textbook. In the graphic organizer below, write two questions you have about the visuals. As you read about soil conservation, write the answers to your questions.

Q. Where was the Dust Bowl?
A.
Q.
A.

Introduction (p. 74)

1. The thick mass of tough roots at the surface of the soil is called
   _____.

Soil as a Resource (p. 75)

2. Is the following sentence true or false? Natural resources are anything made by humans.

   _____

3. Why is soil one of Earth's most valuable resources?

   _____

   _____

   _____

4. Is the following sentence true or false? It can take hundreds of years to form a few centimeters of soil.

   _____

Weathering and Soil • *Reading/Notetaking Guide*

5. Circle the letter of each sentence that is true about soil.

   a. Soil is a nonrenewable resource.
   b. Soil formation takes a long time.
   c. Fertile soil lacks nutrients.
   d. Half of Earth has soils that are good for farming.

Soil Damage and Loss (pp. 75–76)

6. How can soil be damaged?

   _____

   _____

7. How can soil be lost?

   _____

   _____

8. How can plants protect soil from water erosion?

   _____

   _____

   _____

9. Circle the letter of each sentence that is true about the Great Plains.

   a. The Great Plains have fertile soil.
   b. Rainfall decreases from east to west across the Great Plains.
   c. The Great Plains begin at the Appalachian Mountains.
   d. The Great Plains have never been farmed or used for ranches.

10. Circle the letter of each state that was part of the Dust Bowl.

    a. Oklahoma
    b. Kansas
    c. Texas
    d. Missouri

11. Why did the Dust Bowl occur?

    _____

    _____

    _____

12. Why did the Dust Bowl lead to the adoption of modern methods of saving the soil?

    _____

    _____

    _____

Weathering and Soil · *Reading/Notetaking Guide*

Soil Conservation *(continued)*

Soil Conservation (p. 77)

13. The management of soil to prevent its destruction is referred to as

_____.

14. Complete the Venn diagram.

Two Types of Plowing

a. _____   b. _____

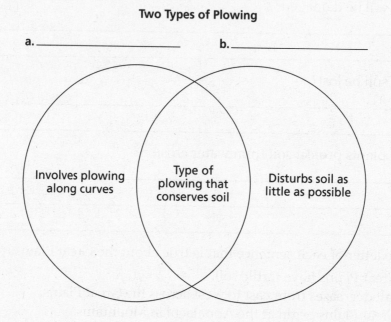

Involves plowing along curves

Type of plowing that conserves soil

Disturbs soil as little as possible

15. How do the two types of plowing in the diagram help conserve soil?

_____

_____

_____

_____

_____

Chapter 3 Erosion and Deposition · *Section 1 Summary*

Changing Earth's Surface

Key Concepts

- What processes wear down and build up Earth's surface?
- What causes the different types of mass movement?

Erosion is the process by which natural forces move weathered rock and soil from one place to another. Gravity, running water, glaciers, waves, and wind all cause erosion. The material moved by erosion is **sediment.** When the agents of erosion lay down sediment, **deposition** occurs. Deposition changes the shape of the land. **Weathering, erosion, and deposition act together in a cycle that wears down and builds up Earth's surface. This cycle, called the geologic cycle, has continued for billions of years.** Erosion and deposition are at work everywhere on Earth.

Gravity pulls everything toward the center of Earth. **Gravity** is the force that moves rock and other materials downhill. Gravity causes **mass movement,** any one of several processes that move sediment downhill. **The different types of mass movement include landslides, mudflows, slump, and creep.** Mass movement can be rapid or slow.

A landslide is a kind of mass movement that occurs when rock and soil slide rapidly down a steep slope. Some landslides contain huge masses of rock, while others may contain only a small amount of rock and soil.

A mudflow is the rapid downhill movement of a mixture of water, rock, and soil. The amount of water in a mudflow can be as high as 60 percent. Mudflows often occur after heavy rains in a normally dry area. In clay soils with a high water content, mudflows may occur even on very gentle slopes. An earthquake can trigger both mudflows and landslides.

A slump is a type of mass movement in which a mass of rock and soil rapidly slips down a slope. It looks as if someone pulled the bottom out from under part of the slope. A slump often occurs when water soaks the base of a mass of soil that is rich in clay.

Creep is the very slow downhill movement of rock and soil. It occurs most often on gentle slopes. Creep often results from the freezing and thawing of water in cracked layers of rock beneath the soil. Creep is so slow that you can barely notice it, but you can see its effects in objects such as telephone poles, gravestones, and fenceposts. Creep may tilt these objects at spooky angles.

Erosion and Deposition • *Reading/Notetaking Guide*

Changing Earth's Surface (pp. 88–91)

This section explains how sediment is carried away and deposited elsewhere to wear down and build up Earth's surface. The section also describes ways that gravity moves sediment downhill.

Use Target Reading Skills

As you read, fill in the graphic organizer below to compare and contrast types of mass movement.

Types of Mass Movement	Speed	Slope
Landslide	a.	b.
Mudflow	c.	d.
Slump	e.	f.
Creep	g.	h.

Wearing Down and Building Up (pp. 88–89)

1. What is erosion?

   _____

   _____

2. List the agents of erosion.

   a. _____   b. _____

   c. _____   d. _____

   e. _____

3. The material moved by erosion is called _____.

4. Where does deposition occur?

   _____

   _____

   _____

Name _____ Date _____ Class _____

Erosion and Deposition • *Reading/Notetaking Guide*

Mass Movement (pp. 89–91)

5. Circle the letter of each sentence that is true about gravity.

    a. It pulls things toward Earth's center.
    b. It causes landslides.
    c. It causes mass movement.
    d. It is an agent of erosion.

6. Is the following sentence true or false? The most destructive kind of mass movement is creep. _____

7. Is the following sentence true or false? Mudflows and slump are especially likely in soils high in clay. _____

8. Complete the concept map.

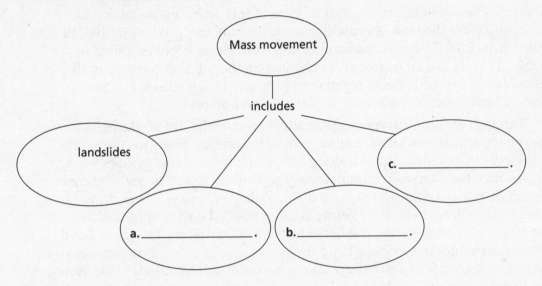

    d. Write a sentence that explains the relationship among the concepts shown.

    _____

    _____

    _____

Match the type of mass movement with its description.

	Mass Movement	**Description**
_____	**9.** landslide	**a.** Rock and soil suddenly slip down a slope in one large mass.
_____	**10.** mudflow	
_____	**11.** slump	**b.** Rock and soil slide quickly down a steep slope.
_____	**12.** creep	**c.** Rock and soil move very slowly downhill.
		d. A mixture of water, rock, and soil moves rapidly downhill.

Chapter 3 Erosion and Deposition ▪ *Section 2 Summary*

Water Erosion

Key Concepts

- What process is mainly responsible for shaping the surface of the land?

- What features are formed by water erosion and deposition?

- What factors affect a river's ability to erode and carry sediment?

Water running downhill is the major agent of erosion that has shaped Earth's land surface. The force of a falling raindrop can loosen and pick up soil particles. As water moves over land, it carries these particles with it. This moving water is called **runoff,** which is water that moves over Earth's surface. The amount of runoff in an area depends on five main factors: amount of rain, amount of vegetation, type of soil, shape of the land, and how people use the land. As runoff travels, it forms tiny grooves in the soil called **rills.** Rills flow into one another and form larger grooves, called gullies. A **gully** is a large groove, or channel, in the soil that carries runoff after a rainstorm. Gullies join together to form streams. A **stream** is a channel along which water is continually flowing down a slope.

Through erosion, a river creates valleys, waterfalls, flood plains, meanders, and oxbow lakes. A river's water has energy. **Energy** is the ability to do work or cause change. All along a river, the water's energy does work. Rivers often form on steep mountain slopes. There, a river generally follows a straight, narrow course, creating a deep, V-shaped valley. Lower down, a river usually flows over more gently sloping land. The river spreads out, forming a wide river valley. The flat, wide area of land along a river is a **flood plain.** A **meander** is a looplike bend in the course of a river. Sometimes a meandering river forms an **oxbow lake,** a meander that has been cut off from the river.

As water moves, it carries sediment with it. Whenever moving water slows down, it deposits sediment. **Deposition creates landforms such as alluvial fans and deltas. It can also add soil to a river's flood plain.** When a river flows out of a mountain valley, the water slows down. Then sediments are deposited in an **alluvial fan,** a wide, sloping deposit formed where a stream leaves a mountain range. A river ends when it flows into a still body of water, such as an ocean or a lake. There the water slows down and deposits sediment. This sediment builds up a landform called a **delta.** Deposition also occurs during floods.

The ability of a river to cause erosion and carry sediment depends on several factors. **A river is a dynamic system. A river's slope, volume of flow, and the shape of its streambed all affect how fast the river flows and how much sediment it can erode.** The amount of sediment that a river carries is its **load.**

Erosion and Deposition · *Reading/Notetaking Guide*

Water Erosion (pp. 94–103)

This section describes how moving water erodes and deposits sediment to create landforms such as valleys and deltas.

Use Target Reading Skills

Read the section "Alluvial Fans" on page 99 in your textbook. Complete the following flowchart showing the steps in the formation of an alluvial fan.

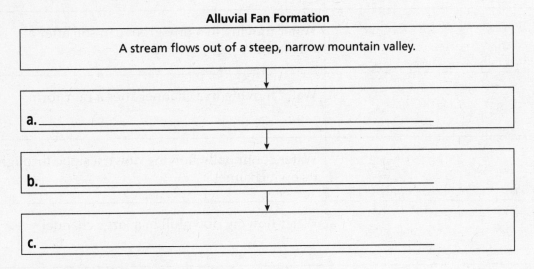

Alluvial Fan Formation

A stream flows out of a steep, narrow mountain valley.

a. _____

b. _____

c. _____

Runoff and Erosion (pp. 95–96)

1. Water running downhill is the major agent of _____.

2. Water that moves over Earth's surface when it rains is called

   _____.

3. Other than how people use the land, list four factors that determine the amount of runoff in an area.

   a. _____   b. _____

   c. _____   d. _____

4. Is the following sentence true or false? More runoff generally means less erosion. _____

Erosion and Deposition ▪ *Reading/Notetaking Guide*

Water Erosion *(continued)*

5. Fill in the first column of the table with the correct form of moving water.

Forms of Moving Water	
Form	**Description**
a.	Water moving in a tiny groove in soil after a rainstorm
b.	Water moving in a channel after a rainstorm
c.	Water continually flowing down a slope through its own channel
d.	Water flowing downhill in a large channel

    e. Which form of moving water causes the greatest changes in the shape of the land? Explain.

_____

_____

6. Unlike gullies, streams rarely _____.

7. A large stream is also called a(n) _____.

Erosion by Rivers (pp. 96–98)

8. How do V-shaped valleys form?

_____

_____

_____

9. When does a river develop meanders?

_____

_____

10. A meander that has been cut off from a river is called a(n)
_____.

Name _____ Date _____ Class _____

11. Identify and label each of the following landforms in the illustration: waterfall, oxbow lake, meander, flood plain, and V-shaped valley.

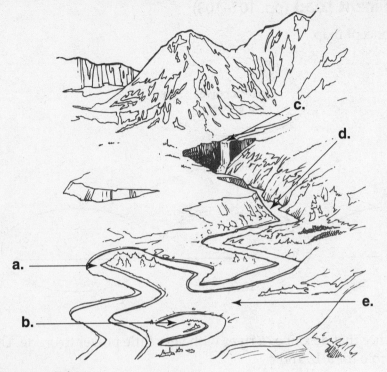

Deposits by Rivers (pp. 98–101)

12. List two landforms created from deposits by rivers.

    a. _____   b. _____

13. What is an alluvial fan?

    _____

    _____

    _____

14. Sediments deposited where a river flows into an ocean or lake form a(n)

    _____.

15. What makes a river valley fertile?

    _____

    _____

Erosion and Deposition · *Reading/Notetaking Guide*

Water Erosion *(continued)*

Erosion and Sediment Load (pp. 102–103)

16. Complete the concept map.

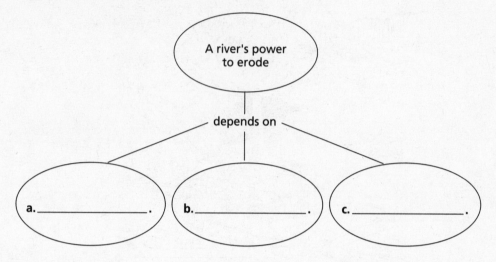

    d. Write a sentence that describes a river with very little power to erode. Use the terms you wrote for a, b, and c.

    _____

    _____

    _____

17. Is the following sentence true or false? When a river slows down and deposits its sediment load, smaller particles of sediment are deposited first. _____

Erosion and Deposition ▪ *Reading/Notetaking Guide*

18. Circle the letter of each factor that increases the speed of a river.

    a. steep slope
    b. low volume
    c. deep streambed
    d. boulders in streambed

19. Circle the letter of each factor that decreases the speed of a river.

    a. gentle slope
    b. high volume
    c. shallow streambed
    d. boulders in streambed

20. Is the following sentence true or false? Where a river flows in a straight line, the water flows faster along the river's sides than near its center.

    _____

21. Label the drawing to show where the river erodes sediment and where it deposits sediment as it flows around the curve.

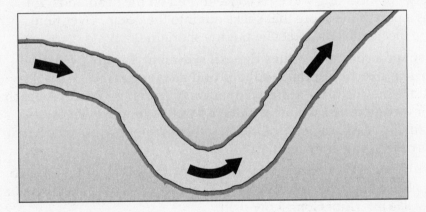

Waves and Wind

Key Concepts

- What gives waves their energy?

- How do waves shape a coast?

- What are the causes and effects of wind erosion?

Ocean waves contain energy—sometimes a great deal of energy. **The energy in waves comes from wind that blows across the water's surface.**

Waves are a major force of erosion along coasts. **Waves shape the coast through erosion by breaking down rock and transporting sand and other sediment.** When large waves hit the shore, their energy can break apart rocks.

Waves also erode by abrasion. When a sediment-carrying wave hits land, the sediment wears away rock like sandpaper wearing away wood.

The energy of incoming waves is concentrated on the headlands. A **headland** is a part of the shore that sticks out into the ocean. Over time, waves erode the headlands and even out the shoreline.

Waves shape a coast when they deposit sediment, forming coastal features such as beaches, spits, sandbars, and barrier beaches. As waves reach the shore, they drop the sediment they carry, forming a beach. A **beach** is an area of wave-washed sediment along a coast. As angled waves repeatedly hit the beach, some of the beach sediment moves down the beach in a process called **longshore drift.**

One result of longshore drift is the formation of a spit. A **spit** is a beach that projects like a finger out into the water. Spits occur where a headland or another obstacle interrupts longshore drift.

Incoming waves carrying sand may build up sandbars, which are long ridges of sand parallel to shore. A barrier beach is similar to a sand bar.

A **sand dune** is a deposit of wind-blown sand. Wind is the weakest agent of erosion. Yet wind can be a powerful force in shaping the land in areas where there are few plants to hold the soil in place.

Wind causes erosion by deflation and abrasion. Geologists define **deflation** as the process by which wind removes surface materials. Deflation does not usually have a great effect on the land. In deserts, though, deflation can sometimes create an area of rock fragments called desert pavement. Abrasion by wind-carried sand can polish rock, but it causes little erosion.

All sediment picked up by wind eventually falls to the ground. This happens when wind slows down or some obstacle, such as a boulder or clump of grass, traps the windblown sand and other sediment. **Wind erosion and deposition may form sand dunes and loess deposits.** Sand dunes can be seen on beaches and in deserts where windblown sediment has built up. Sediment that is finer than sand is sometimes deposited in layers far from its source. This fine, wind-deposited sediment is **loess.**

Erosion and Deposition ▪ *Reading/Notetaking Guide*

Waves and Wind (pp. 108–114)

This section explains how waves form and describes the erosion and deposition that waves cause. This section also describes how wind causes erosion and discusses the types of deposits that are caused by wind.

Use Target Reading Skills

As you read about waves, complete the graphic organizer by filling in the details.

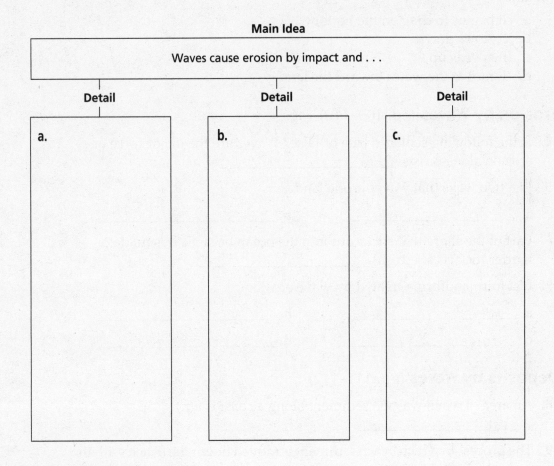

Main Idea

Waves cause erosion by impact and . . .

Detail   **Detail**   **Detail**

a.

b.

c.

How Waves Form (p. 108)

1. Circle the letter of each sentence that is true about the energy in waves.
   a. It comes from wind.
   b. It moves water particles up and down.
   c. It moves water particles forward.
   d. It moves across the water.

Erosion and Deposition • *Reading/Notetaking Guide*

Waves and Wind (continued)

2. What part of the water is affected by a wave in deep water?

   _____

   _____

   _____

3. Circle the letter of each sentence that is true about a wave approaching land.

   a. It begins to drag on the bottom.
   b. It slows down.
   c. It speeds up.
   d. It moves the water toward the land.

Erosion by Waves (pp. 109–110)

4. Is the following sentence true or false? Waves are the major force of erosion along coasts. _____

5. List two ways that waves erode land.

   a. _____   b. _____

6. Part of the shore that sticks out into the ocean because it is made of harder rock is called a(n) _____.

7. List four landforms created by wave erosion.

   a. _____   b. _____

   c. _____   d. _____

Deposits by Waves (pp. 111–112)

8. An area of wave-washed sediment along a coast is a(n)
   _____.

9. The process in which beach sediment is moved down the beach with the current is called _____.

10. How does a spit form?

    _____

    _____

    _____

Erosion and Deposition · *Reading/Notetaking Guide*

Erosion by Wind (pp. 112–113)

11. A deposit of wind-blown sand is a(n) _____.

12. Is the following sentence true or false? Wind is the strongest agent of erosion. _____

13. Why is wind effective in causing erosion in deserts?

_____

_____

_____

14. Circle the letter of each sentence that is true about deflation.
    a. It is the main way wind causes erosion.
    b. It usually has a great effect on the land.
    c. It can create blowouts.
    d. It can create desert pavement.

15. Circle the letter of each sentence that is true about abrasion by wind-carried sand.
    a. It can polish rock.
    b. It causes little erosion.
    c. It causes most desert landforms.
    d. It causes most erosion.

Deposition by Wind (p. 114)

16. Is the following sentence true or false? All the sediment picked up by wind eventually falls to the ground. _____

17. When does wind-carried sediment fall to the ground?

_____

_____

_____

18. List two types of deposits formed by wind erosion and deposition.

    a. _____   b. _____

Erosion and Deposition · *Reading/Notetaking Guide*

Waves and Wind *(continued)*

19. Complete the Venn diagram by adding the following phrases: have finer sediments, have coarser sediments, result from wind erosion.

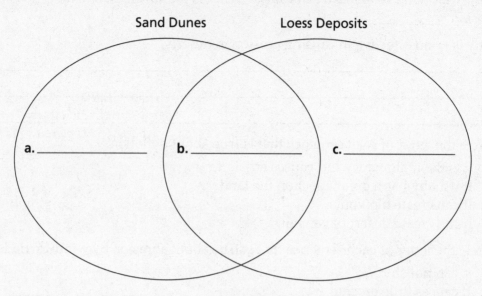

Sand Dunes   Loess Deposits

a. _____   b. _____   c. _____

d. Which type of sediment can be found far from its source? Explain.

_____

_____

Glaciers

Key Concepts

- What are the two kinds of glaciers?
- How does a valley glacier form and move?
- How do glaciers cause erosion and deposition?

A **glacier** is any large mass of ice that moves slowly over land. **There are two kinds of glaciers—continental glaciers and valley glaciers.** A **continental glacier** is a glacier that covers much of a continent or large island. Today, continental glaciers cover about 10 percent of Earth's land, including Antarctica and most of Greenland. Continental glaciers can flow in all directions.

Many times in the past, continental glaciers have covered large parts of Earth's surface. These times are known as **ice ages.** Beginning about 2.5 million years ago, continental glaciers advanced and retreated, or melted back, several times. They finally retreated about 10,000 years ago. A **valley glacier** is a long, narrow glacier that forms when snow and ice build up high in a mountain valley. Valley glaciers are found on many high mountains.

Glaciers can form only in an area where more snow falls than melts. Once the depth of snow and ice reaches more than 30 to 40 meters, gravity begins to pull the glacier downhill. Valley glaciers move, or flow, at a rate of a few centimeters to a few meters per day. Sometimes a valley glacier slides down more quickly in what is called a surge.

The movement of a glacier changes the land beneath it. Although glaciers work slowly, they are a major force of erosion. **The two processes by which glaciers erode the land are plucking and abrasion.** As a glacier flows over the land, it picks up rocks in a process called **plucking.** Plucking can move even huge boulders. Many rocks remain on the bottom of a glacier, and the glacier drags them across the land. This process, called abrasion, gouges and scratches the bedrock.

A glacier gathers huge amounts of rock and soil as it moves. **When a glacier melts, it deposits the sediment it eroded from the land, creating various landforms.** The mixture of sediments that a glacier deposits directly on the surface is called **till.** The till deposited at the edges of a glacier forms a ridge called a **moraine.** A terminal moraine is the ridge of till at the farthest point reached by a glacier. Retreating glaciers also create features called kettles. A **kettle** is a small depression that forms when a chunk of ice is left in glacial till. When the ice melts, the kettle remains. A kettle that is filled with water is called a kettle lake.

Name _____ Date _____ Class _____

Glaciers (pp. 115–119)

This section describes huge ice masses, called glaciers. The section also describes the ice ages, a time when glaciers covered much of Earth. In addition, the section explains how glaciers form and move and how they cause erosion and deposition.

Use Target Reading Skills

Read the section "How Glaciers Shape the Land" on page 117 in your textbook. Complete the following flowchart showing the steps of glacial erosion.

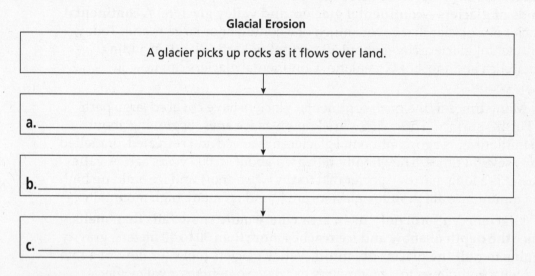

Glacial Erosion

A glacier picks up rocks as it flows over land.

↓

a. _____

↓

b. _____

↓

c. _____

How Glaciers Form and Move (p. 116)

1. Any large mass of ice that moves slowly over land is a(n) _____ .

2. Circle the letter of each sentence that is true about continental glaciers.
    a. They are larger than valley glaciers.
    b. They spread out over wide areas.
    c. They are found only in Antarctica.
    d. They cover almost half of Earth's land.

3. What are ice ages?

    _____

    _____

    _____

4. Is the following sentence true or false? The most recent ice age ended about 10,000 years ago. _____

5. Is the following sentence true or false? All of North America was covered by a continental glacier in the last ice age. _____

Erosion and Deposition • *Reading/Notetaking Guide*

6. Circle the letter of each sentence that is true about valley glaciers.
   a. They are generally long, narrow glaciers.
   b. They are found on many high mountains.
   c. They are larger than continental glaciers.
   d. They usually move down valleys.

7. Where can glaciers form?

   _____

   _____

8. When does the snow and ice that make up a glacier begin to move downhill?

   _____

   _____

   _____

9. Complete the table to show how the different types of glaciers move.

How Glaciers Move	
Type of Glacier	**How It Moves**
a.	Flows in all directions
b.	Flows in a surge

   c. Relate the movement of continental glaciers to why they cover Antarctica and most of Greenland.

   _____

   _____

   _____

How Glaciers Shape the Land (pp. 117–119)

10. List two processes by which glaciers erode the land.

    a. _____   b. _____

11. Is the following sentence true or false? Plucking can move only small stones. _____

Erosion and Deposition • *Reading/Notetaking Guide*

Glaciers *(continued)*

12. Describe abrasion and how it affects bedrock.

_____

_____

_____

_____

13. When does a glacier deposit the sediment it is carrying?

_____

_____

_____

Match each type of glacial landform with its description.

Type of Landform	**Description**
____ **14.** till	**a.** Small depression formed by a chunk of ice when it melts
____ **15.** moraine	
____ **16.** terminal moraine	**b.** Mixture of sediments a glacier deposits on the surface
____ **17.** drumlin	**c.** Ridge formed at the edge of a glacier
____ **18.** kettle	**d.** Long mound of till that is smoothed in the direction of the glacier's flow
____ **19.** cirque	
____ **20.** arête	**e.** Ridge at the farthest point reached by a glacier
____ **21.** fiord	**f.** Sharp ridge separating two cirques
	g. Bowl-shaped hollow eroded by a glacier
	h. Sea-filled valley cut by a glacier in a coastal region

22. Explain the difference between glacial erosion and glacial deposition.

_____

_____

_____

_____

_____

_____

Chapter 4 Plate Tectonics · *Section 1 Summary*

Earth's Interior

Key Concepts

■ How have geologists learned about Earth's inner structure?

■ What are the characteristics of Earth's crust, mantle, and core?

Earth's surface is constantly changing. Earth looks different today from the way it did millions of years ago. People wonder, "What's inside Earth?" The extreme conditions in Earth's interior prevent exploration far below the surface. **Geologists have used two main types of evidence to learn about Earth's interior: direct evidence from rock samples and indirect evidence from seismic waves.**

Rocks from inside Earth give geologists clues about Earth's structure. Geologists can make inferences about conditions deep inside Earth where these rocks formed. Using data from **seismic waves** produced by earthquakes, geologists have learned that Earth's interior is made up of several layers.

The three main layers of Earth are the crust, the mantle, and the core. These layers vary greatly in size, composition, temperature, and pressure. Beneath the surface, the temperature remains the same for about 20 meters, then increases until the center of Earth is reached. **Pressure** results from a force pressing on an area. Pressure inside Earth increases as you go deeper.

The **crust** is the layer of rock that forms Earth's outer skin. **The crust is a layer of solid rock that includes both dry land and the ocean floor.** Oceanic crust consists mostly of rocks such as basalt, dark rock with a fine texture. Continental crust, the crust that forms the continents, consists mainly of rocks such as granite. Granite is a rock that usually is a light color and has a coarse texture.

Below a boundary about 40 kilometers beneath the surface is the solid material of the **mantle,** a layer of hot rock. **Earth's mantle is made up of rock that is very hot, but solid. Different layers of the mantle have different physical characteristics.** The uppermost part of the mantle and the crust together form a rigid layer called the **lithosphere.** Below the lithosphere is a soft layer called the **asthenosphere.** Beneath the asthenosphere, the mantle is solid. This solid material, called the lower mantle, extends all the way to Earth's core.

The core is made mostly of the metals iron and nickel. It consists of two parts—a liquid outer core and a solid inner core. The **outer core** is a layer of molten metal that surrounds the inner core. The **inner core** is a dense ball of solid metal.

Scientists think that movements in the liquid outer core create Earth's magnetic field. Because Earth has a magnetic field, the planet acts like a giant bar magnet.

Earth's Interior (pp. 132–139)

This section explains how scientists learn about Earth's interior. The section also describes the layers that make up Earth and explains why Earth acts like a giant magnet.

Use Target Reading Skills

Preview the red heading Earth's Interior *and the blue subheadings* Evidence from Rock Samples, *and* Evidence from Seismic Waves. *Complete the graphic organizer below by answering the question that is asked about each heading.*

Earth's Interior

Heading	Question	Answer
Evidence from Rock Samples	What did scientists learn about Earth's interior by studying rock samples?	a.
Evidence from Seismic Waves	How did evidence from seismic waves help scientists learn about Earth's interior?	b.

Exploring Inside Earth (p. 133)

1. What prevents geologists from directly exploring Earth's interior?

_____

_____

2. Geologists use direct evidence from _____ to learn about Earth's interior.

3. Geologists learn about Earth's interior using indirect evidence from

_____.

Plate Tectonics ▪ *Reading/Notetaking Guide*

4. Is the following sentence true or false? Geologists are able to drill to the center of Earth. _____

5. Seismic waves reveal the structure of Earth through their _____ and _____.

6. Circle the letter of each sentence that is true about Earth.

   a. Indirect evidence of Earth's interior comes from studying rock samples.
   b. Geologists cannot observe Earth's interior directly.
   c. It is over 6,000 kilometers from the surface to the center of Earth.
   d. Geologists learn about Earth's interior by drilling holes.

7. _____ waves are produced by earthquakes.

A Journey to the Center of Earth (p. 134)

8. How does the temperature change as you go from the surface toward the center of Earth?

   _____

   _____

   _____

9. How does pressure change as you go from the surface toward the center of Earth?

   _____

   _____

10. The three main layers that make up Earth are the _____, _____, and _____.

The Crust (p. 135)

11. The _____ is a layer of rock that forms Earth's outer skin.

12. Is the following sentence true or false? The crust is thinnest under high mountains. _____

13. The dark-colored rock that makes up most of the oceanic crust is

   _____.

14. The light-colored rock that makes up most of the continental crust is

   _____.

Earth's Interior (*continued*)

The Mantle (pp. 136–137)

Match the name of each layer of the mantle with its description.

Layer	Description
____ 15. lower mantle	a. Rigid layer that includes the upper part of the mantle and the crust
____ 16. lithosphere	b. Solid material beneath the asthenosphere
____ 17. asthenosphere	c. Soft layer just below the lithosphere

18. Is the following sentence true or false? The asthenosphere is not considered solid because it can bend like plastic. _____

19. Is the following sentence true or false? The mantle is nearly 3,000 kilometers thick. _____

The Core (pp. 138–139)

20. Circle the letter of each sentence that is true about Earth's outer core.

    a. It is under low pressure.
    b. It is made of solid metal.
    c. It contains iron and nickel.
    d. It is a solid.

21. Circle the letter of each sentence that is true about Earth's inner core.

    a. It consists of molten metal.
    b. It is a thick liquid.
    c. It is not very dense.
    d. It is under extreme pressure.

22. In the drawing, label the three main layers of Earth.

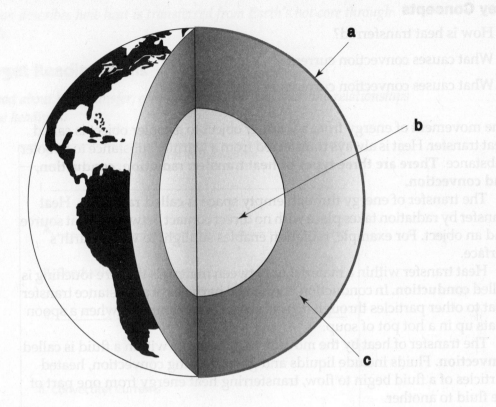

a

b

c

23. Describe how a compass needle aligns itself.

_____

_____

_____

24. What creates Earth's magnetic field?

_____

_____

_____

Plate Tectonics · *Reading/Notetaking Guide*

Convection and the Mantle (continued)

4. What are two forms of radiation?

_____

_____

5. What is conduction?

_____

_____

6. What is an example of conduction?

_____

_____

_____

7. What is convection?

_____

_____

_____

8. Heat transfer by convection is caused by differences of _____ and density within a fluid.

9. A measure of how much mass there is in a volume of a substance is _____.

10. Circle the letter of the sentence that describes what happens to a fluid when its temperature increases.

   a. Its particles occupy less space.
   b. Its density decreases.
   c. Its particles move more slowly.
   d. Its particles settle together more closely.

Convection Currents (p. 142)

11. What three factors set convection currents in motion?

_____

_____

12. What happens to convection currents when the liquid or gas is no longer heated?

_____

_____

_____

Plate Tectonics ▪ *Reading/Notetaking Guide*

Convection Currents in Earth (p. 143)

13. Complete the graphic organizer to show the relationships among heat, movement, and density in mantle rock.

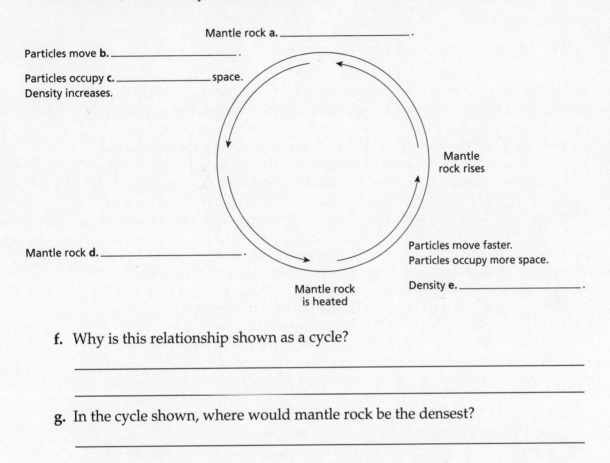

Mantle rock **a.** _____ .

Particles move **b.** _____ .

Particles occupy **c.** _____ space.
Density increases.

Mantle
rock rises

Mantle rock **d.** _____ .

Particles move faster.
Particles occupy more space.

Mantle rock
is heated

Density **e.** _____ .

f. Why is this relationship shown as a cycle?

_____

_____

g. In the cycle shown, where would mantle rock be the densest?

_____

_____

14. Is the following sentence true or false? The heat source for the convection currents in the mantle is the sun. _____

Drifting Continents

Key Concepts

■ What was Alfred Wegener's hypothesis about the continents?

■ What evidence supported Wegener's hypothesis?

■ Why was Alfred Wegener's hypothesis rejected by most scientists of his day?

In 1910, a young German scientist named Alfred Wegener became curious about why the coasts of several continents matched so well, like the pieces of a jigsaw puzzle. He formed a hypothesis that Earth's continents had moved! **Wegener's hypothesis was that all the continents were once joined together in a single landmass and have since drifted apart.** He named this supercontinent **Pangaea,** meaning "all lands." According to Wegener, Pangaea existed about 300 million years ago. Over tens of millions of years, Pangaea began to break apart. The pieces of Pangaea slowly moved toward their present-day locations, becoming the continents of today. The idea that the continents slowly moved over Earth's surface became known as **continental drift. Wegener gathered evidence from different scientific fields to support his ideas about continental drift. He studied land features, fossils, and evidence of climate change.** In a book called *The Origin of Continents and Oceans,* Wegener presented his evidence.

Mountain ranges and other features provided evidence for continental drift. For example, Wegener noticed that when he pieced together maps of Africa and South America, a mountain range running from east to west in Africa lines up with a range in South America. Also, European coal fields match up with coal fields in North America.

Fossils also provided evidence to support Wegener's theory. A **fossil** is any trace of an ancient organism that has been preserved in rock. The fossils of the reptiles *Mesosaurus* and *Lystrosaurus* and a fernlike plant called *Glossopteris* have been found on widely separated landmasses. This convinced Wegener that the continents had once been united.

Wegener used evidence from climate change to further support his theory. For example, an island in the Arctic Ocean contains fossils of tropical plants. According to Wegener, the island once must have been located close to the equator. Wegener also pointed to scratches on rocks in South Africa that were made by glaciers. These scratches show that the mild climate of South Africa was once cold enough for glaciers to form. According to Wegener's theory, Earth's climate has not changed. Instead, the positions of the continents have changed.

Wegener also attempted to explain how the drift of continents took place. **Unfortunately, Wegener could not provide a satisfactory explanation for the force that pushes or pulls the continents.** Because he could not identify the cause of continental drift, most geologists rejected his theory. For nearly half a century, from the 1920s to the 1960s, most scientists paid little attention to the idea of continental drift. Then new evidence about Earth's structure led scientists to reconsider Wegener's bold theory.

Plate Tectonics ▪ *Reading/Notetaking Guide*

Drifting Continents (pp. 144–148)

This section describes a hypothesis of how the continents came to be located where they are today. The section also gives evidence for the hypothesis and explains why the hypothesis was not accepted for many years.

Use Target Reading Skills

As you read about the evidence that supports the hypothesis of continental drift, complete the graphic organizer.

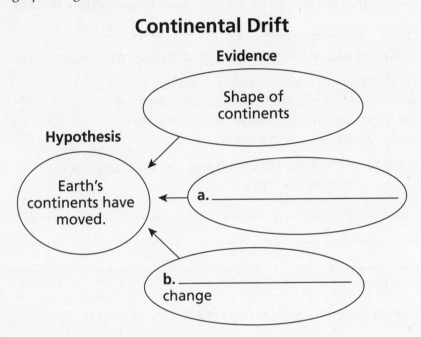

Continental Drift

Evidence

Hypothesis

Shape of continents

Earth's continents have moved.

a. _____

b. _____
change

Continental Drift (pp. 145–147)

1. State Alfred Wegener's hypothesis about how Earth's continents have moved.

   _____

   _____

   _____

   _____

2. Wegener named his supercontinent _____.

Plate Tectonics ▪ *Reading/Notetaking Guide*

Drifting Continents *(continued)*

3. What did Wegener think had happened to this supercontinent?

_____

_____

_____

_____

4. Wegener's idea that the continents slowly moved over Earth's surface

became known as _____.

5. Circle the letter of each sentence that supports Wegener's hypothesis.

   a. Some continents match up like jigsaw puzzle pieces.
   b. Different rock structures are found on different continents.
   c. Fossils of tropical plants are found near the equator.
   d. Continental glaciers once covered South Africa.

6. Give an example of evidence from land features that supported
   Wegener's idea of continental drift.

_____

_____

_____

_____

7. Any trace of an ancient organism preserved in rock is called a(n)

_____.

8. How did Wegener explain similar fossils on different continents?

_____

_____

_____

_____

9. Is the following sentence true or false? Wegener believed that
   continental drift explained fossils of tropical plants found in places that
   today have a polar climate. _____

Plate Tectonics ▪ *Reading/Notetaking Guide*

Wegener's Hypothesis Rejected (p. 148)

10. How did Wegener think that mountains formed?

_____

_____

_____

_____

_____

11. How do the locations of mountains support Wegener's idea about how mountains form?

_____

_____

_____

_____

_____

Chapter 4 Plate Tectonics • *Section 4 Summary*

Sea-Floor Spreading

Key Concepts

- What is the process of sea-floor spreading?
- What is the evidence for sea-floor spreading?
- What happens at deep-ocean trenches?

The longest chain of mountains in the world is the system of **mid-ocean ridges.** In the mid-1900s, scientists mapped the mid-ocean ridges using sonar. **Sonar** is a device that bounces sound waves off underwater objects and then records the echoes of these sound waves. The mid-ocean ridges curve along the sea floor, extending into all of Earth's oceans. Most of the mountains in the mid-ocean ridges lie hidden under hundreds of meters of water. A steep-sided valley splits the top of some mid-ocean ridges.

Earth's ocean floors move, carrying the continents along with them. This movement begins at a mid-ocean ridge. A ridge forms along a crack in the oceanic crust. At a mid-ocean ridge, molten material rises from the mantle and erupts. This process, called **sea-floor spreading,** continually adds new material to the ocean floor. **In sea-floor spreading, the sea floor spreads apart along both sides of a mid-ocean ridge as new crust is added. As a result, the ocean floors move like conveyor belts, carrying the continents along with them.**

Several types of evidence supported the theory of sea-floor spreading: eruptions of molten material, magnetic stripes in the rock of the ocean floor, and the ages of the rocks themselves. Scientists have found strange rocks shaped like pillows in the central valley of mid-ocean ridges. Such rocks can form only if molten material hardens quickly after erupting under water. The presence of these rocks supports the theory of sea-floor spreading. More support came when scientists discovered that ocean floor rock lies in a pattern of magnetized "stripes." The pattern is the same on both sides of the ridge. These stripes hold a record of reversals in Earth's magnetic field. The final proof of sea-floor spreading came from ocean floor rock samples. The farther from a ridge the rocks were taken, the older they were.

The ocean floor does not just keep spreading. Instead, it sinks into deep underwater canyons called **deep-ocean trenches.** Where there are trenches, subduction takes place. **Subduction** is the process by which the ocean floor sinks into a deep-ocean trench and back into the mantle. **In a process taking tens of millions of years, part of the ocean floor sinks back into the mantle at deep-ocean trenches.**

The processes of subduction and sea-floor spreading can change the size and shape of the oceans. Because of these processes, the ocean floor is renewed about every 200 million years. The Pacific Ocean is shrinking. Its many trenches are swallowing more ocean crust than the mid-ocean ridge is producing. The Atlantic Ocean is expanding. In most places, the oceanic crust of the Atlantic Ocean is attached to continental crust. As the Atlantic's floor spreads, the continents along its edges also move.

Plate Tectonics · *Reading/Notetaking Guide*

Sea-Floor Spreading (pp. 149–155)

This section explains sea-floor spreading and describes evidence supporting its occurrence. The section also explains subduction and describes how subduction affects Earth's oceans.

Use Target Reading Skills

As you read about the evidence that supports the hypothesis of sea-floor spreading, complete the graphic organizer.

Sea-Floor Spreading Results

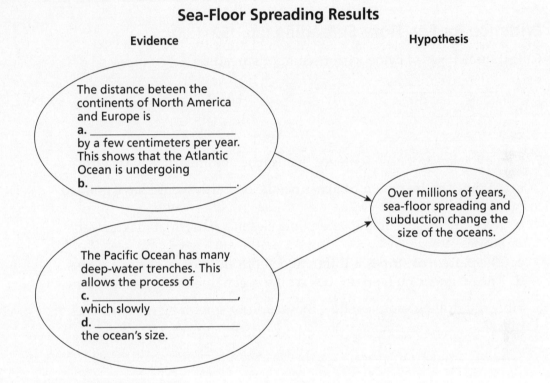

Evidence

Hypothesis

The distance beteen the continents of North America and Europe is
a. _____
by a few centimeters per year. This shows that the Atlantic Ocean is undergoing
b. _____.

The Pacific Ocean has many deep-water trenches. This allows the process of
c. _____,
which slowly
d. _____
the ocean's size.

Over millions of years, sea-floor spreading and subduction change the size of the oceans.

Mid-Ocean Ridges (p. 150)

1. Circle the letter of each sentence that is true about mid-ocean ridges.

   a. The mid-ocean ridges were mapped using sonar.
   b. The mid-ocean ridges are found only below the Pacific Ocean.
   c. The mid-ocean ridges are completely under water.
   d. The tops of some mid-ocean ridges are split by a steep-sided valley.

2. A device that bounces sound waves off underwater objects is called

   _____.

3. What is sonar used for?

   _____

   _____

Plate Tectonics • *Reading/Notetaking Guide*

Sea-Floor Spreading *(continued)*

What Is Sea-Floor Spreading? (p. 151)

4. The process that continually adds new material to the ocean floor is called _____.

5. In sea-floor spreading, where does new crust come from?

_____

_____

Evidence for Sea-Floor Spreading (pp. 152–153)

6. List three types of evidence for sea-floor spreading.

   a. _____

   b. _____

   c. _____

7. Circle the letter of each sentence that is true about Earth's magnetism.

   a. At times in the past, a compass needle on Earth would have pointed south.
   b. Rock that makes up the ocean floor lies in a pattern of magnetized stripes.
   c. The pattern of stripes is different on both sides of mid-ocean ridges.
   d. The magnetic memory of rock on the ocean floor changes over time.

8. How did drilling samples show that sea-floor spreading really has taken place?

_____

_____

_____

_____

Plate Tectonics · *Reading/Notetaking Guide*

Subduction at Trenches (pp. 154–155)

9. A long, narrow and very deep canyon where the ocean floor bends down toward the mantle is called a _____ .

10. What is subduction?

   _____

   _____

   _____

11. Complete the cause, events, and effect graphic organizer to show the relationships among the processes of convection currents, subduction, and sea-floor spreading.

a._____ in Earths mantle

   ↓

b._____

   results in ↓

The ocean is changed in c._____

   d. What process in Earth's interior causes subduction and sea-floor spreading?

   _____

   _____

   e. What effect do those two events have on Earth's surface?

   _____

   _____

12. Is the following sentence true or false? At deep-ocean trenches, conduction allows oceanic crust to sink back into the mantle.

   _____

13. Is the following sentence true or false? The Pacific Ocean is shrinking.

   _____

14. Why is the Atlantic Ocean expanding?

   _____

   _____

   _____

The Theory of Plate Tectonics

Key Concepts

- What is the theory of plate tectonics?

- What are the three types of plate boundaries?

Earth's lithosphere is broken into separate sections called **plates.** The plates fit closely together along cracks in the crust. They carry the continents, or parts of the ocean floor, or both. **Plate tectonics** is the geological theory that states that pieces of Earth's lithosphere are in slow, constant motion, driven by convection currents in the mantle. A scientific theory is a well-tested concept that explains a wide range of observations. **The theory of plate tectonics explains the formation, movement, and subduction of Earth's plates.**

The plates float on top of the asthenosphere. Convection currents rise in the asthenosphere and spread out beneath the lithosphere, causing the movement of Earth's plates. As the plates move, they produce changes in Earth's surface, including volcanoes, mountain ranges, and deep-ocean trenches. The edges of different pieces of the lithosphere meet at lines called plate boundaries. **Faults**—breaks in Earth's crust where rocks have slipped past each other—form along these boundaries.

There are three kinds of plate boundaries: spreading boundaries, colliding boundaries, and sliding boundaries. The plates move at amazingly slow rates, from about 1 to 24 centimeters per year. They have been moving for tens of millions of years. The place where two plates move apart, or diverge, is called a **spreading boundary.** Most spreading boundaries occur at the mid-ocean ridge. When a spreading boundary develops on land, two slabs of Earth's crust slide apart. A deep valley called a **rift valley** forms along the spreading boundary. The place where two plates come together, or converge, is a **colliding boundary.** When two plates converge, the result is called a collision. When two plates collide, the density of the plates determines which one comes out on top. Oceanic crust is more dense than continental crust. A **sliding boundary** is a place where two plates slip past each other, moving in opposite directions. Earthquakes occur frequently along these boundaries.

When two plates carrying oceanic crust meet at a trench, the plate that is less dense dives under the other plate and returns to the mantle. This is the process of subduction. When a plate carrying oceanic crust collides with a plate carrying continental crust, the more dense oceanic plate plunges beneath the continental plate through the process of subduction. When two plates carrying continental crust collide, subduction does not take place because both plates are mostly low-density granite rock. Instead, the plates collide head-on. The collision squeezes the crust into mighty mountain ranges.

About 260 million years ago, the continents were joined together in the supercontinent Pangaea. About 225 million years ago, Pangaea began to break apart. Since then, the continents have moved to their present locations.

Plate Tectonics ▪ *Reading/Notetaking Guide*

The Theory of Plate Tectonics (pp. 158–162)

This section explains how the lithosphere is broken into separate sections that move.

Use Target Reading Skills

Look at the illustration titled Plate Tectonics *on pages 160–161 of your textbook. In the graphic organizer below, ask three questions that you have about the illustration. As you read about plate tectonics, write answere to your questions.*

Plate Tectonics

Q. What are the three types of plate boundaries?
A.
Q. What happens at colliding boundaries?
A.
Q. What happens at spreading boundaries?
A.
Q. What happens at sliding boundaries?
A.

Plate Tectonics ▪ *Reading/Notetaking Guide*

The Theory of Plate Tectonics *(continued)*

Introduction (p. 158)

1. The lithosphere is broken into separate sections called

    _____.

2. Is the following sentence true or false? Plates can carry continents or parts
    of the ocean floor but not both. _____

3. What is a scientific theory?

    _____

    _____

    _____

    _____

    _____

    _____

    _____

    _____

How Plates Move (p. 159)

4. State the theory of plate tectonics.

    _____

    _____

    _____

    _____

    _____

    _____

    _____

    _____

5. Is the following sentence true or false? The theory of plate tectonics
    explains the formation, movement, and subduction of Earth's plates.

    _____

Plate Tectonics • *Reading/Notetaking Guide*

Plate Boundaries (pp. 160–162)

Match the term with its definition.

Term	Definition
____ 6. plate boundary	**a.** Deep valley that forms where two plates pull apart
____ 7. fault	**b.** Line where the edges of Earth's plates meet
____ 8. rift valley	**c.** Break in Earth's crust where rocks have slipped past each other

9. Complete the compare/contrast table to explain how plates move at the different types of plate boundaries.

Plate Movement	
Type of Plate Boundary	**How Plates Move**
Spreading boundary	**a.**
Colliding boundary	**b.**
Sliding boundary	**c.**

    d. How are the movement of plates at divergent boundaries and at sliding boundaries similar?

_____

_____

_____

10. Is the following sentence true or false? Crust is neither created nor destroyed along a sliding boundary. _____

11. Most spreading boundaries occur along _____.

Plate Tectonics ▪ *Reading/Notetaking Guide*

The Theory of Plate Tectonics *(continued)*

12. When two plates collide, what determines which plate comes out on top?

_____

_____

13. Circle the letter of each sentence that is true about colliding boundaries.

    a. Where two plates carrying oceanic crust meet, subduction does not take place.

    b. An oceanic plate sinks beneath a continental plate when the two plates collide.

    c. Where two plates meet, the one that is more dense sinks under the other.

    d. Mountain ranges form where two plates carrying continental crust collide.

14. Was Pangaea the only supercontinent to have existed? Explain your answer.

_____

_____

_____

15. Is the following sentence true or false? The pieces of the supercontinent Pangaea began to drift apart about 225 million years ago.

_____

16. What does computer modeling show about the breakup of Pangaea?

_____

_____

_____

Chapter 5 Earthquakes · *Section 1 Summary*

Forces in Earth's Crust

Key Concepts

- How does stress in the crust change Earth's surface?

- Where are faults usually found, and why do they form?

- What land features result from the forces of plate movement?

The movement of Earth's plates creates enormous forces that squeeze or pull the rock in the crust. A force that acts on rock to change its shape or volume is **stress.** Stress adds energy to the rock. The energy is stored in the rock until it changes shape or breaks.

Three different kinds of stress can occur in the crust. **Tension, compression, and shearing work over millions of years to change the shape and volume of rock. Tension** pulls on the crust, stretching rock so that it becomes thinner in the middle. **Compression** squeezes rock until it folds or breaks. **Shearing** pushes a mass of rock in two opposite directions.

When enough stress builds up in rock, the rock breaks, creating a fault. A fault is a break in the rock of the crust where rock surfaces slip past each other. **Most faults occur along plate boundaries, where the forces of plate motion push or pull the crust so much that the crust breaks. There are three main types of faults: normal faults, reverse faults, and strike-slip faults.**

Tension causes a normal fault. In a **normal fault,** the fault is at an angle, and one block of rock lies above the fault while the other block lies below the fault. The block of rock that lies above is called the **hanging wall.** The rock that lies below is called the **footwall.** Compression causes reverse faults. A **reverse fault** has the same structure as a normal fault, but the blocks move in the opposite direction. Shearing creates strike-slip faults. In a **strike-slip fault,** the rocks on either side of the fault slip past each other sideways, with little up or down motion.

Over millions of years, the forces of plate movement can change a flat plain into landforms produced by folding, stretching, and uplifting Earth's crust. These landforms include anticlines and synclines, folded mountains, fault-block mountains, and plateaus. A fold in rock that bends upward into an arch is an anticline. A fold in rock that bends downward to form a valley is a syncline. Anticlines and synclines are found on many parts of the Earth's surface where compression forces have folded the crust. The collision of two plates can cause compression and folding of the crust over a wide area. When two normal faults cut through a block of rock, fault movements may push up a fault-block mountain. The forces that raise mountains can also uplift, or raise plateaus. A **plateau** is a large area of flat land elevated high above sea level.

Earthquakes · *Reading/Notetaking Guide*

Forces in Earth's Crust (pp. 174–180)

This section explains how stresses in Earth's crust cause breaks, or faults, in the crust. The section also explains how faults and folds in Earth's crust form mountains.

Use Target Reading Skills

Review the text in the section "Normal Faults" on page 176. Complete the chart below by identifying the main idea of the section along with three important details about the topic.

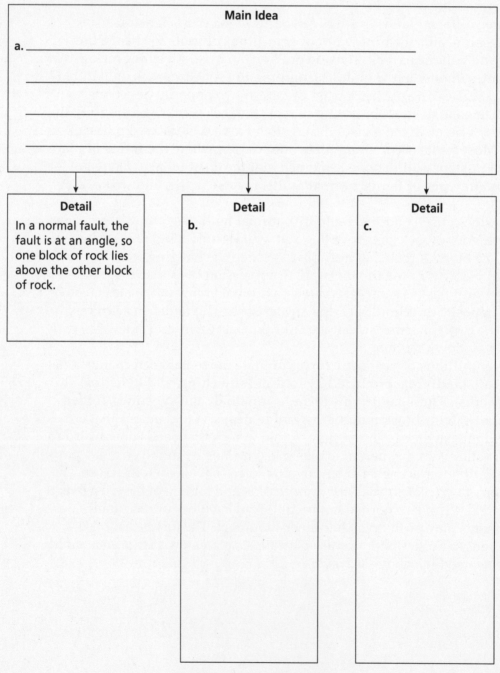

Main Idea

a. _____

_____

_____

_____

Detail

In a normal fault, the fault is at an angle, so one block of rock lies above the other block of rock.

Detail

b.

Detail

c.

Earthquakes · *Reading/Notetaking Guide*

Introduction (p. 174)

1. Circle the letter of the term that refers to force that acts on rock to change its shape or volume.

   a. fault   **b.** stress   **c.** pressure   **d.** heat

2. The amount of space a rock takes up is its _____.

Types of Stress (p. 175)

3. List the three types of stress that occur in Earth's crust.

   a. _____

   b. _____

   c. _____

4. Complete the cause-event-effect chart to show how the different types of stress change the shape and volume of rock.

Cause	Event	Effect
Tension	c.	e.
a.	d.	Rock folds or breaks
b.	Pushes rock in two different directions	f.

   g. Which type of stress causes the crust to become thinner?

   _____

Kinds of Faults (pp. 176–177)

5. A break in Earth's crust is a(n) _____.

Match the kind of fault with its description.

Type of Fault

____ 6. strike-slip fault

____ 7. normal fault

____ 8. reverse fault

Description

a. The hanging wall slides up and over the footwall.

b. There is little up or down motion.

c. The hanging wall slips downward below the footwall.

Earthquakes · *Reading/Notetaking Guide*

Forces in Earth's Crust *(continued)*

9. Is the following sentence true or false? A strike-slip fault that forms the boundary between two plates is called a convergent boundary.

_____

10. Circle the letter of each sentence that is true about a hanging wall.

    a. It slips downward when movement occurs along a normal fault.
    b. It is the half of a fault that lies below in a reverse fault.
    c. It is the same as a footwall.
    d. It occurs when the fault is at an angle.

11. Circle the letter of each sentence that is true about both normal and reverse faults.

    a. The faults are at an angle.
    b. The faults are caused by tension.
    c. The faults are caused by compression.
    d. The faults have footwalls.

12. Complete the flowchart to show the types of faults and movements caused by stress on rock.

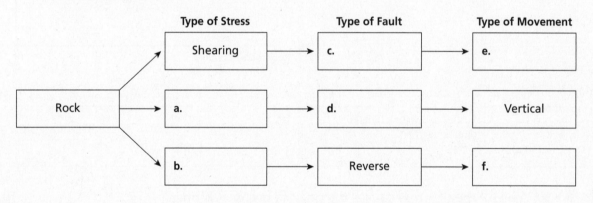

Earthquakes · *Reading/Notetaking Guide*

Match the landform with the type of fault or faults found there.

Landform	Type of Fault
____ **13.** San Andreas fault	**a.** reverse fault
____ **14.** Owens valley	**b.** strike-slip fault
____ **15.** Klamath Mountains	**c.** normal fault

Changing Earth's Surface (pp. 178–180)

Match the term with its definition.

Term	Definition
____ **16.** anticline	**a.** Fold in rock that bends upward
____ **17.** syncline	**b.** Fold in rock that bends downward

18. Circle the letter of the sentence that describes how a fault-block mountain is created.

  a. It is created by two normal faults.
  b. It is created by two reverse faults.
  c. It is created by a strike-slip fault.
  d. It is created by shearing.

19. Circle the letter of each mountain range that was caused at least in part by folding.

  a. Alps
  b. Himalayas
  c. Coast Range
  d. Great Basin

20. What is a plateau?

  _____

  _____

Earthquakes and Seismic Waves

Key Concepts

■ How does the energy of an earthquake travel through Earth?

■ What are the scales used to measure the strength of an earthquake?

■ How do scientists locate the epicenter of an earthquake?

An **earthquake** is the shaking that results from the movement of rock beneath Earth's surface. The area beneath Earth's surface where rock under stress breaks to cause an earthquake is called the **focus.** The point on the surface directly above the focus is called the **epicenter.** During an earthquake, vibrations called seismic waves move out from the focus in all directions. **Seismic waves carry energy from an earthquake away from the focus, through Earth's interior, and across the surface.**

There are three categories of seismic waves: P waves, S waves, and surface waves. **P waves** compress and expand the ground like an accordion. **S waves** vibrate from side to side and up and down. When P waves and S waves reach the surface, some become surface waves. **Surface waves** move more slowly than P waves and S waves, but they can produce severe ground movements.

There are three commonly used methods of measuring earthquakes: the Mercalli scale, the Richter scale, and the moment magnitude scale. The **Mercalli scale** was developed to rate earthquakes according to the level of damage at a given place. An earthquake's **magnitude** is a number that geologists assign to an earthquake based on the earthquake's strength. The **Richter scale** is a rating of an earthquake's magnitude based on the size of the earthquake's seismic waves. The seismic waves are measured by a **seismograph.** A seismograph is an instrument that records and measures seismic waves. Geologists today often use the **moment magnitude scale,** a rating system that estimates the total energy released by an earthquake. An earthquake's magnitude tells geologists how much stored energy was released by the earthquake. The effects of an earthquake increase with magnitude.

Geologists use seismic waves to locate an earthquake's epicenter. When an earthquake strikes, P waves arrive at a seismograph first and S waves next. The farther away the epicenter is, the greater the difference between the two arrival times. This time difference tells scientists how far from the seismograph the epicenter is. The scientists then use the information from three different seismograph stations to plot circles on a map. Each circle shows the distance from one seismograph station to all the points where the epicenter could be located. The single point where the three circles intersect is the location of the earthquake's epicenter.

Earthquakes · *Reading/Notetaking Guide*

Earthquakes and Seismic Waves (pp. 181–187)

This section explains how energy from an earthquake travels through Earth, how it can be detected, and how the size of an earthquake can be measured.

Use Target Reading Skills

As you read about seismic waves, complete the graphic organizer by filling in the details.

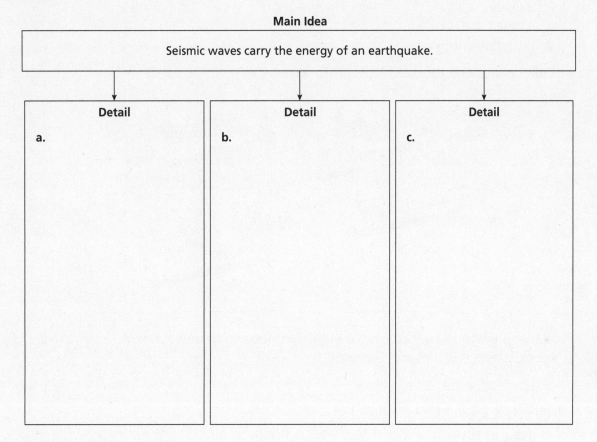

Main Idea

Seismic waves carry the energy of an earthquake.

Detail

a.

Detail

b.

Detail

c.

Introduction (p. 181)

1. The area where rock under stress breaks and triggers an earthquake

   is called the _____.

2. The point on the surface directly above the focus is the

   _____.

Types of Seismic Waves (pp. 182–183)

3. What are seismic waves?

   _____

   _____

Earthquakes · *Reading/Notetaking Guide*

Earthquakes and Seismic Waves (continued)

4. Is the following sentence true or false? Seismic waves carry the energy of an earthquake away from the focus in all directions.

   _____

5. Circle the letter of each term that is a category of seismic wave.

   a. P wave
   b. S wave
   c. surface wave
   d. underground wave

6. Label each drawing as *S Waves* or *P Waves*.

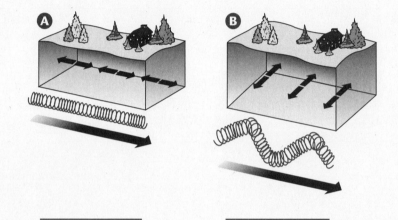

   _____   _____

7. Is the following sentence true or false? Surface waves move more quickly than P waves and S waves.

   _____

Match the type of wave with its effect.

Type of Wave	Effect
____ 8. P wave	a. shakes buildings from side to side
____ 9. S wave	b. shakes structures violently
____ 10. Surface wave	c. causes the ground to compress and expand

Earthquakes • *Reading/Notetaking Guide*

Measuring Earthquakes (pp. 184–186)

11. An instrument that records and measures seismic waves is a(n)

    _____.

12. List the three scales that are used for measuring earthquakes.

    a. _____

    b. _____

    c. _____

13. In your own words, write a definition of each earthquake scale.

    a. _____

    _____

    _____

    b. _____

    _____

    _____

    _____

    c. _____

    _____

    _____

Locating the Epicenter (pp. 186–187)

14. Is the following sentence true or false? The closer an earthquake, the greater the time between the arrival of P waves and the arrival of S waves.

    _____

15. Geologists use circles to find the epicenter of an earthquake.

    a. What does the center of each circle represent?

    _____

    b. What does the radius of each circle represent?

    _____

Chapter 5 Earthquakes ▪ *Section 3 Summary*

Monitoring Earthquakes

Key Concepts

- How do seismographs work?

- How do geologists monitor faults?

- How are seismographic data used?

Many societies have used technology to try to determine when and where earthquakes have occurred. During the late 1800s, scientists developed seismographs that were much more sensitive and accurate than any earlier devices. A simple seismograph can consist of a heavy weight attached to a frame by a spring or wire. A pen connected to the weight rests its point on a drum that can rotate. As the drum rotates slowly, the pen draws a straight line on paper that is wrapped tightly around the drum. **Seismic waves cause the seismograph's drum to vibrate. But the suspended weight with the pen attached moves very little. Therefore, the pen stays in place and records the drum's vibrations.** The pattern of lines, called a **seismogram,** is the record of an earthquake's seismic waves produced by a seismograph.

To monitor faults, geologists have developed instruments to measure changes in elevation, tilting of the land surface, and ground movements along faults. A tiltmeter measures tilting or raising of the ground. A creep meter uses a wire stretched across a fault to measure horizontal movement of the ground. A laser-ranging device uses a laser beam to detect horizontal fault movements. A network of Earth-orbiting satellites called GPS (global positioning system) helps scientists monitor changes in elevation and tilt of the land as well as horizontal movement along faults.

Seismographs and fault-monitoring devices provide data used to map faults and detect changes along faults. Geologists are also trying to use these data to develop a method of predicting earthquakes. Geologists use the data from seismic waves to map faults, which are often hidden by a thick layer of rock or soil. This practice helps geologists determine the earthquake risk for an area. Geologists use fault-monitoring devices to study the types of movement that occur along faults. **Friction** is the force that opposes the motion of one surface as it moves across another surface. Where friction along a fault is low, the rocks on both sides of the fault slide by each other without much sticking. Stress does not build up, and large earthquakes are unlikely. Where friction is high, the rocks lock together. Stress builds up until an earthquake occurs. Even with data from many sources, geologists can't predict when and where a quake will strike.

Earthquakes • *Reading/Notetaking Guide*

Monitoring Earthquakes (pp. 190–195)

This section explains how geologists monitor faults to try to predict earthquakes.

Use Target Reading Skills

Review the text in the section "Trying to Predict Earthquakes" on page 195. Complete the chart below by identifying two details that support the main idea.

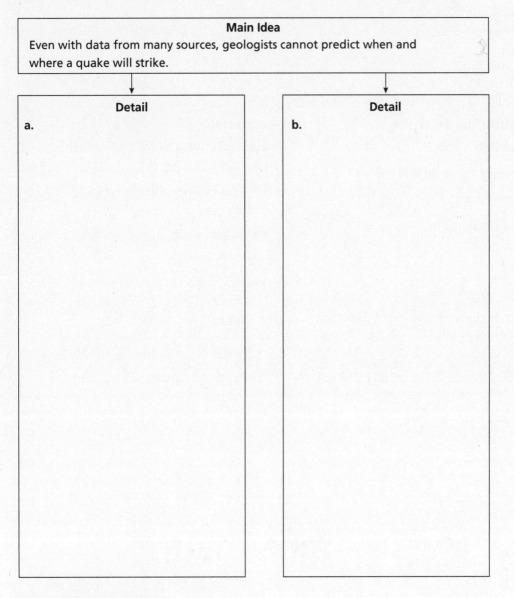

Main Idea
Even with data from many sources, geologists cannot predict when and where a quake will strike.

Detail
a.

Detail
b.

The Seismograph (p. 191)

1. After an earthquake, in what order are the different types of seismic waves recorded by a seismograph?

_____

_____

Earthquakes • *Reading/Notetaking Guide*

Monitoring Earthquakes *(continued)*

Instruments That Monitor Faults *(pp. 192–193)*

2. List four instruments that geologists use to monitor movements along faults.

    a. _____

    b. _____

    c. _____

    d. _____

Match the type of monitoring device with its description.

Monitoring Device	**Description**
____ **3.** creep meter	**a.** Uses a network of Earth-orbiting satellites
____ **4.** laser-ranging device	**b.** Detects changes in distance to a reflector
____ **5.** tiltmeter	**c.** Measures movement along a slip-strike fault
____ **6.** GPS satellite	**d.** Works like a carpenter's level

7. Label each circle in the Venn diagram with the name of the monitoring device it represents.

a. _____   **b.** _____

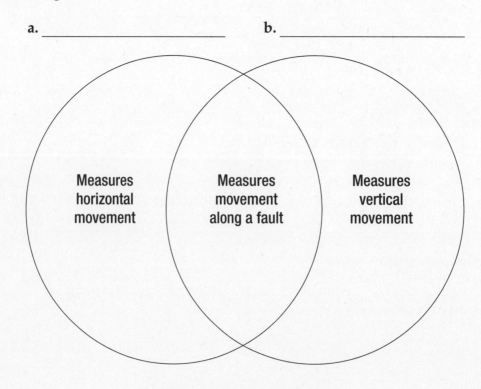

Measures horizontal movement

Measures movement along a fault

Measures vertical movement

Earthquakes • *Reading/Notetaking Guide*

8. A device that bounces laser beams off a reflector to detect fault

   movements is a(n) _____.

9. A device that can measure tiny vertical or horizontal movements of
   markers set up on the opposite sides of a fault is a(n)

   _____.

Using Seismographic Data (pp. 194–195)

10. How do seismic waves behave when they encounter a fault?

   _____

   _____

   _____

   _____

11. How do the data from the movements of seismic waves help geologists
    determine the earthquake risk for an area?

   _____

   _____

   _____

   _____

12. The force that opposes the motion of one surface as it moves across

    another surface is referred to as _____.

13. Is the following sentence true or false? Geologists can predict accurately
    where and when an earthquake will strike.

   _____

Chapter 5 Earthquakes ▪ *Section 4 Summary*

Earthquake Safety

Key Concepts

- How do geologists determine earthquake risk?

- What kinds of damage does an earthquake cause?

- What can be done to increase earthquake safety and reduce earthquake damage?

Geologists can determine earthquake risk by locating where faults are active, where past earthquakes have occurred, and where the most damage was caused. In the United States, the risk is highest along the Pacific Coast in the states of California, Washington, and Alaska. The eastern United States generally has a low risk of earthquakes. Geologists use Mercalli scale data to produce intensity maps. These maps show the areas most likely to suffer serious earthquake damage. Geologists also study where earthquakes have occurred in the past to help determine earthquake risk.

    Causes of earthquake damage include shaking, liquefaction, aftershocks, and tsunamis. The shaking produced by seismic waves can trigger landslides or avalanches. The types of rock and soil determine where and how much the ground shakes. **Liquefaction** occurs when an earthquake's violent shaking suddenly turns loose, soft soil into liquid mud. As the ground gives way, buildings sink and pull apart. Sometimes, buildings weakened by an earthquake collapse during an aftershock. An **aftershock** is an earthquake that occurs after a larger earthquake in the same area.

    When an earthquake jolts the ocean floor, plate movement causes the ocean floor to rise slightly and push water out of its way. The water displaced by the earthquake may form a large wave called a **tsunami.** A tsunami spreads out from an earthquake's epicenter and speeds across the ocean. The height of the wave is low in the open ocean, but the wave grows into a mountain of water as the tsunami approaches shallow water.

    The main danger from earthquake strikes is from falling objects and flying glass. **The best way to protect yourself is to drop, cover, and hold.** To prepare for an earthquake, store in a convenient location an earthquake kit containing canned food, water, and first aid supplies.

    Most earthquake-related deaths and injuries result from damage to buildings or other structures. **To reduce earthquake damage, new buildings must be made stronger and more flexible. Older buildings may be modified to withstand stronger quakes.** The way in which a building is constructed determines whether it can withstand an earthquake. A **base-isolated building** is designed to reduce the amount of energy that reaches the building during an earthquake. During a quake, the building moves gently back and forth without any violent shaking.

    Earthquakes can cause fire and flooding when gas pipes and water mains break. Flexible joints and automatic shut-off valves can be installed to prevent breaking and to cut off gas and water flow.

Earthquakes · *Reading/Notetaking Guide*

Earthquake Safety (pp. 196–202)

This section explains how earthquakes cause damage. The section also describes how buildings can be constructed to withstand earthquakes and what people can do to help protect themselves from earthquakes.

Use Target Reading Skills

Complete the first column in the chart by filling in the red headings. Then in the second column, ask a what, how, *or* where *question for each heading. As you read the section, complete the third column with the answers.*

Section 4: Earthquake Safety		
Heading	Question	Answer
	Where is quake risk highest?	Earthquake risk is highest . . .

Earthquake Safety *(continued)*

Earthquake Risk (pp. 197–198)

1. What three factors do geologists use to determine earthquake risk?

_____

_____

_____

2. Circle the letter of the location where the risk of earthquakes is highest in the United States.

   a. along the Gulf of Mexico   **b.** along the Atlantic Coast
   c. along the Great Lakes   **d.** along the Pacific Coast

3. Which scale provides data for intensity maps of earthquake damage?

   a. Richter scale   **b.** Mercalli scale
   c. Wegener scale   **d.** moment magnitude scale

How Earthquakes Cause Damage (pp. 199–200)

4. What kinds of damage are caused by the severe shaking of an earthquake?

_____

_____

_____

_____

5. What determines where and how much the ground shakes?

_____

6. Is the following sentence true or false? A house built on solid rock will shake more during an earthquake than a house built on sandy soil.

_____

7. The process in which an earthquake's violent shaking turns loose, soft soil into liquid mud is called _____. This process is likely to occur where the soil is full of

_____.

8. An earthquake that occurs after a larger earthquake in the same area is referred to as a(n) _____.

9. Large ocean waves usually caused by strong earthquakes below the ocean floor are called _____.

Earthquakes · *Reading/Notetaking Guide*

Steps to Earthquake Safety (p. 200)

10. What is the main danger to people during an earthquake?

    _____

11. Is the following sentence true or false? If no desk or table is available, you should crouch against an inner wall.

    _____

12. Is the following sentence true or false? If you are outdoors during an earthquake, you should move to an open area.

    _____

Designing Safer Buildings (pp. 201–202)

13. How can tall furniture be prevented from tipping over in an earthquake?

    _____

    _____

14. How can bedrooms be made safer during an earthquake?

    _____

    _____

15. How can a brick or wood-frame building be modified to help it withstand an earthquake?

    _____

    _____

    _____

16. What can be done when a new home is being built to help prevent damage caused by liquefaction?

    _____

    _____

17. How does a base-isolated building reduce the amount of energy that reaches the building during an earthquake?

    _____

    _____

18. How can earthquakes cause fire and flooding?

    _____

    _____

Chapter 6 Volcanoes · *Section 1 Summary*

Volcanoes and Plate Tectonics

Key Concepts

- Where are most of Earth's volcanoes found?

- How do hot spot volcanoes form?

A **volcano** is a weak spot in the crust where molten material, or magma, comes to the surface. **Magma** is a molten mixture of rock-forming substances, gases, and water from the mantle. When magma reaches the surface, it is called **lava.** When lava has cooled, it forms solid rock. Lava released during volcanic activity builds up Earth's surface.

Volcanoes occur in belts that extend across continents and oceans. One major volcanic belt is the **Ring of Fire,** formed by the many volcanoes that rim the Pacific Ocean. **Volcanic belts form along the boundaries of Earth's plates.** At plate boundaries, huge pieces of the crust spread apart or collide. As a result, the crust often fractures, allowing magma to reach the surface. Most volcanoes form along spreading plate boundaries such as mid-ocean ridges and along colliding plate boundaries where subduction takes place. Along the rift valley, lava pours out of cracks in the ocean floor, gradually building new mountains.

Many volcanoes form near colliding plate boundaries where oceanic plates return to the mantle. Volcanoes may form where two oceanic plates collide or where an oceanic plate collides with a continental plate. Many volcanoes occur near boundaries where two oceanic plates collide. Through subduction, the older, denser plate sinks into a deep-ocean trench down into the mantle. Some of the rock above the subducting plate melts and forms magma. Because the magma is less dense than the surrounding rock, it rises toward the surface. Eventually, the magma breaks through the ocean floor, creating volcanoes. The resulting volcanoes create a string of islands called an **island arc.** Volcanoes also occur where an oceanic plate is subducted beneath a continental plate.

Some volcanoes result from "hot spots" in Earth's mantle. A **hot spot** is an area where material from within the mantle rises and then melts, forming magma. **A volcano forms above a hot spot when magma erupts through the crust and reaches the surface.** A hot spot on the ocean floor can gradually form a series of volcanic mountains. The Hawaiian Islands formed one by one over millions of years as the Pacific plate drifted over a hot spot. Hot spots can also form under the continents. Yellowstone National Park in Wyoming marks a hot spot under the North American plate.

Volcanoes • *Reading/Notetaking Guide*

Volcanoes and Plate Tectonics (pp. 216–219)

This section explains what volcanoes are and identifies where most volcanoes occur.

Use Target Reading Skills

Complete the first column in the chart by filling in the red headings. Then in the second column, ask a what, how, *or* where *question for each heading. As you read the section, complete the third column with answers.*

Section 1 : Volcanoes and Plate Tectonics		
Heading	**Question**	**Answer**
	Where do volcanoes occur?	Most volcanoes occur in belts that extend across oceans and continents.

Introduction (p. 216)

1. What is a volcano?

   _____

   _____

   _____

2. A molten mixture of rock-forming substances, gases, and water from the mantle is referred to as _____.

3. When magma reaches the surface, it is called _____.

Volcanoes • *Reading/Notetaking Guide*

Volcanoes and Plate Tectonics (continued)
Volcanoes and Plate Boundaries (pp. 217–218)

4. What is the Ring of Fire?

_____

_____

_____

5. Where do most volcanoes form?

_____

_____

_____

6. Describe how volcanoes form along the mid-ocean ridges.

_____

_____

_____

7. Is the following sentence true or false? Volcanoes can form along spreading plate boundaries on land.

_____

8. Is the following sentence true or false? Many volcanoes form near colliding plate boundaries where oceanic crust returns to the mantle.

_____

9. How does subduction at colliding plate boundaries lead to the formation of volcanoes?

_____

_____

_____

10. Volcanoes at boundaries where two oceanic plates collide create a string of islands called a(n) _____.

11. List three major island arcs.

_____

_____

Volcanoes · *Reading/Notetaking Guide*

12. Circle the letter of the types of plates that collided to form the Andes Mountains on the west coast of South America.

    a. two oceanic plates
    b. a continental plate and an oceanic plate
    c. a continental plate and an island plate
    d. two continental plates

Hot Spot Volcanoes (p. 219)

13. What is a hot spot?

    _____

    _____

    _____

    _____

14. How did the Hawaiian Islands form?

    _____

    _____

    _____

    _____

15. Is the following sentence true or false? Hot spots form only under oceanic crust.

    _____

Volcanic Eruptions

Key Concepts

- What happens when a volcano erupts?

- What are the two types of volcanic eruptions?

- What are a volcano's stages of activity?

Lava begins as magma deep beneath Earth's surface. Magma flows upward through cracks in the rock until it becomes trapped or reaches the surface to form a volcano.

Inside a volcano, magma collects in a pocket called a **magma chamber.** The magma moves through a **pipe,** a long tube that connects the magma chamber to Earth's surface. There, the magma leaves the volcano through an opening called a **vent.** The area covered by lava as it pours out of a vent is called a **lava flow.** Lava may collect in a **crater,** a bowl-shaped area around a volcano's central vent. As magma rises toward the surface, the pressure decreases and the dissolved gases begin to expand and exert an enormous force. **When a volcano erupts, the force of the expanding gases pushes magma from the magma chamber through the pipe until it flows or explodes out of the vent.**

Geologists classify volcanic eruptions as quiet or explosive. Silica is a material found in magma that is made of oxygen and silicon. If the magma has a low silica content, it flows easily and the volcano erupts quietly. The gases bubble out gently and the lava oozes quietly. Quiet eruptions can produce both fast-moving, hot lava that is thin and runny (pahoehoe) and slower-moving, cool, thicker lava (aa). A volcano erupts explosively if its magma is high in silica. The thick magma does not flow out of the chamber, but builds up in the pipe. The trapped gases build up pressure until they explode with incredible force. A **pyroclastic flow** occurs when an explosive eruption hurls out ash, cinders, and bombs. Volcano hazards include lava flows, clouds of ash and deadly gases, landslides, and avalanches of mud, snow, or rock.

Geologists often use the terms *active*, *dormant*, **or** *extinct* **to describe a volcano's stage of activity.** An active volcano is one that is erupting or has shown signs that it may erupt in the near future. A **dormant** volcano is not active now but may become active in the future. An **extinct** volcano is unlikely to erupt again. Geologists monitor changes in and around volcanoes to try to predict eruptions. But geologists cannot be certain about the type of eruption or how powerful it will be.

Hot springs and geysers are often found in areas of present or past volcanic activity. Hot springs collect in a natural pool. A **geyser** is a fountain of water and steam that erupts from the ground.

Volcanic Eruptions (pp. 221–228)

This section explains how volcanoes erupt and describes types of volcanic eruptions as well as other types of volcanic activity. The section also describes how geologists monitor volcanoes and what hazards are associated with volcanoes.

Use Target Reading Skills

As you read pages 221–223, complete the outline on volcanic eruptions.

Volcanic Eruptions

I. Magma Reaches Earth's Surface

    A. Inside a Volcano

        1. Magma collects in a _____.

        2. _____ moves up to Earth's surface in a pipe.

        3. Molten rock and gas leave the volcano through a _____.

        4. An area covered by lava as it pours from a vent is a _____.

        5. A _____ is a bowl-showed area that may form at the top
        of a volcano around a central vent.

    B. Volcanic Eruption

        1. Dissolved _____ under pressure are trapped in magma underground.

        2. Gases expand as magma rises to Earth's _____.

        3. The force of the expanding gases pushes magma until it _____
        of a vent on the surface

Introduction (p. 221)

1. Is the following sentence true or false? Magma forms deep beneath Earth's surface.

    _____

2. Is the following sentence true or false? Liquid magma rises until it reaches the surface, or until it becomes trapped beneath layers of rock.

    _____

Volcanic Eruptions *(continued)*

Magma Reaches Earth's Surface *(pp. 222–223)*

3. Circle the letter of each feature that all volcanoes share.

    a. pocket of magma beneath the surface
    b. crack to the surface
    c. side vents
    d. crater

4. Label the drawing with the following terms: magma chamber, pipe, vent, and crater.

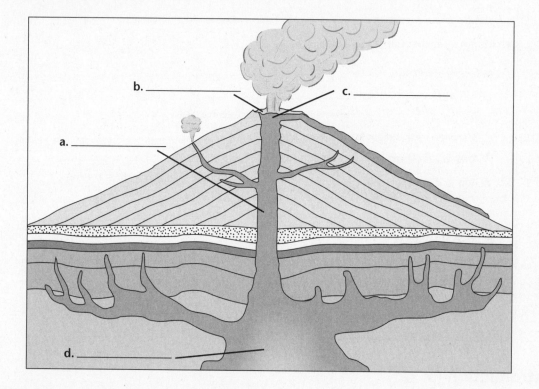

5. What is a lava flow?

_____

_____

6. Where does a crater form?

_____

7. Is the following sentence true or false? The pipe of a volcano is a horizontal crack in the crust.

_____

Volcanoes ▪ *Reading/Notetaking Guide*

8. Complete the flowchart showing in what sequence magma moves
   through a volcano.

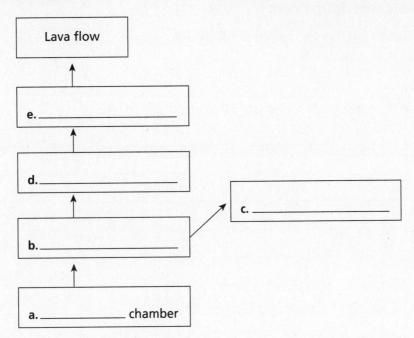

   Lava flow

   e. _____

   d. _____

   c. _____

   b. _____

   a. _____ chamber

   f. What does the flowchart show about where magma goes after it
   leaves the pipes?

   _____

   _____

9. Circle the letter of the sentence that describes the best model of a volcano
   erupting.

   a. Carbon dioxide dissolved in soda pop rushes out when the pop is
   opened.
   b. A car goes faster when the accelerator is pushed.
   c. Water in a pot gets hotter when the pot is heated on a stove.
   d. Clay hardens when it is baked in an oven.

10. What happens during a volcanic eruption?

   _____

   _____

   _____

11. What factors determine the force of a volcanic eruption?

   _____

   _____

Volcanic Eruptions *(continued)*

Kinds of Volcanic Eruptions (pp. 224–226)

12. Is the following sentence true or false? A volcano erupts quietly if its magma is thick and sticky.

_____

13. Complete the table to describe the different types of lava.

	Lava Type	
	Pahoehoe	Aa
Temperature	a.	b.
Appearance	c.	d.
Consistency	e.	f.
Speed of movement	g.	h.

Match the type of lava with its description.

Type of Lava

_____ **14.** volcanic ash

_____ **15.** cinders

_____ **16.** bombs

Description

a. Pebble-sized particles

b. Particles ranging from the size of a baseball to the size of a car

c. Fine rocky particles as small as a speck of dust

17. What is a pyroclastic flow?

_____

_____

18. Is the following sentence true or false? Volcanic eruptions cause damage only when they are close to the crater's rim.

_____

19. What kinds of damage can volcanoes cause?

_____

_____

_____

Volcanoes • *Reading/Notetaking Guide*

Stages of Volcanic Activity (pp. 227–228)

20. Is the following sentence true or false? The activity of a volcano may last from less than a decade to more than 10 million years.

_____

21. Is the following sentence true or false? Most long-lived volcanoes erupt continuously.

_____

22. Complete the table to describe the different stages of a volcano.

Volcanic Stages	
Stage	**Description**
a.	Unlikely to erupt ever again
active	b.
c.	No longer active but may become active again

    d. Rank the volcanic stages from least likely to erupt to most likely to

       erupt: _____

       _____

23. Is the following sentence true or false? Some types of volcanic activity do not involve the eruption of lava.

_____

24. When groundwater heated by a nearby body of magma rises to the surface and collects in a natural pool, it is called a(n)

_____.

25. A fountain of water and steam that erupts from the ground is referred to

    as a(n) _____.

26. Circle the letter of each sentence that is true about predicting volcanic eruptions.

    a. Geologists are more successful in predicting volcanic eruptions than earthquakes.

    b. There is never any warning when a volcano will erupt.

    c. Geologists can predict how powerful a volcanic eruption will be.

    d. Geologists cannot predict what type of eruption a volcano will produce.

Volcanic Landforms

Key Concepts

- What landforms do lava and ash create?
- How does magma that hardens beneath the surface create landforms?

Some volcanic landforms are formed when lava flows build up mountains and plateaus on Earth's surface. **Volcanic eruptions create landforms made of lava, ash, and other materials. These landforms include shield volcanoes, cinder cone volcanoes, composite volcanoes, and lava plateaus.**

At some places on Earth's surface, thin layers of lava pour out of a vent. More layers of such lava harden on top of previous layers. The layers gradually build a wide, gently sloping mountain called a **shield volcano.** If a volcano's lava is thick, the lava may explode into the air and harden into ash, cinders, and bombs. These materials pile up around the vent, forming a steep, cone-shaped hill or mountain called a **cinder cone.** Sometimes lava flows alternate with explosive eruptions of ash, cinders, and bombs. The alternating layers form a tall, cone-shaped mountain called a **composite volcano.** Some eruptions of thin, runny lava flow out of cracks and travel a long distance before cooling and hardening. Over millions of years, these layers of lava build up over a large area to form a lava plateau.

An enormous eruption may empty a volcano's main vent and magma chamber. With nothing to support it, the top of the mountain collapses inward. The huge hole left by the collapse of a volcanic mountain is called a **caldera.**

Over time, the hard surface of a lava flow breaks down to form soil. Some volcanic soils are among the most fertile soils in the world. People have settled close to volcanoes to take advantage of the fertile soil.

Sometimes magma rises upward through cracks in the crust but does not reach Earth's surface. The magma cools and hardens into rock beneath the surface. **Features formed by magma include volcanic necks, dikes, sills, and batholiths.** A **volcanic neck** forms when magma hardens in a volcano's pipe. The softer rock around the pipe wears away, exposing the hard rock of the volcanic neck. A **dike** forms when magma forces itself across rock layers and hardens. A **sill** forms when magma squeezes between layers of rock and hardens. Dikes and sills are examples of igneous intrusions. An **intrusion** forms when magma hardens underground to form igneous rock. When a large body of magma cools inside the crust, a mass of rock called a **batholith** forms. Smaller bodies of hardened magma can form dome mountains.

Volcanoes · *Reading/Notetaking Guide*

Volcanic Landforms (pp. 229–234)

This section describes landforms and soils that are created by volcanoes, and types of geothermal activity.

Use Target Reading Skills

As you read about volcanic landforms, use the headings to complete the outline below.

Volcanic Landforms
I. Landforms From Lava and Ash
A. Shield Volcanoes
B. _____
C. _____
D. Lava Plateaus
E. _____
F. _____
II. Landforms From Magma
A. _____
B. _____
C. _____

Volcanic Landforms *(continued)*

Landforms From Lava and Ash (pp. 230–232)

1. List four landforms created from lava and ash.

   a. _____

   b. _____

   c. _____

   d. _____

2. Circle the letter of each sentence that is true about shield volcanoes.

   a. They form from many thin layers of lava.
   b. They result from quiet eruptions.
   c. They are very steep mountains.
   d. They are formed from ash, cinders, and bombs.

3. Is the following sentence true or false? The Hawaiian Islands are cinder cone volcanoes.

   _____

4. Name two examples of composite volcanoes.

   _____

   _____

5. Is the following sentence true or false? A composite volcano has both quiet and explosive eruptions.

   _____

Volcanoes · *Reading/Notetaking Guide*

Match the landform with its description.

Landform	Description
____ **6.** shield volcano	**a.** High, level area formed by repeated lava flows
____ **7.** cinder cone	**b.** Mountain formed by lava flows alternating with explosive eruptions
____ **8.** composite volcano	**c.** Cone-shaped mountain formed from ash, cinders, and bombs
____ **9.** lava plateau	**d.** Hole left by the collapse of a volcanic mountain
____ **10.** caldera	**e.** Gently sloping mountain formed by repeated lava flows

11. When volcanic ash breaks down, it releases _____ and

_____, both of which are needed by plants.

Landforms From Magma (pp. 233–234)

12. List four features formed by magma.

    a. _____

    b. _____

    c. _____

    d. _____

Volcanoes ▪ *Reading/Notetaking Guide*

Volcanic Landforms *(continued)*

13. Complete the Venn diagram using the following phrases: forms from magma, forms across rock layers, forms between rock layers.

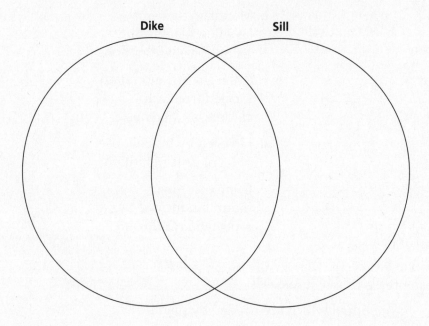

Dike   Sill

14. Dikes and sills are examples of igneous intrusions. An intrusion is always _____ than the rocks around it.

15. A mass of rock formed when a large body of magma cools inside the crust is called a(n) _____.

16. What is an example of a batholith in the United States?

_____

California Geology

Key Concept

■ How does plate tectonics help to explain features of California's geology?

The movements of the Pacific and North American plates produced California's major geological features. These features include faults, volcanoes, mountain ranges, and basins. The large fault system that runs along California's coast was formed as a result of movement along two plate boundaries. The North American plate and the Pacific plate grind past each other with great force. This movement has created many faults that make up the San Andreas fault system.

As oceanic plates get subducted beneath Earth's crust, they melt, forming magma. The magma rises to the surface, forming volcanoes. The volcanoes that have formed along California's coast are the result of active subduction of the Juan de Fuca plate. Mount Shasta and Lassen Peak formed in this way.

California has several mountain ranges. Some of them formed as the result of plate motion. As the Pacific plate and the North American plate collided, some of the crust crumpled and was pushed upward. This formed mountain ranges such as the Sierra Nevada and the Coast and Transverse ranges. Erosion has since shaped them into the peaks we see today.

Sometimes, plate movements cause the crust to warp downward. This forms large bowl-shaped valleys, or **basins.** These valleys often form between mountain ranges in response to the uplifting in the area next to them. Erosion of the surrounding mountains produces the sediment that fills these valleys. The **Central Valley** of California formed in this way.

Name _____ Date _____ Class _____

Volcanoes · *Reading/Notetaking Guide*

California Geology (pp. 235–237)

This section explains the major geological features of California's landscape.

Use Target Reading Skills

As you read about California's Geology, complete the graphic organizer by filling in the details.

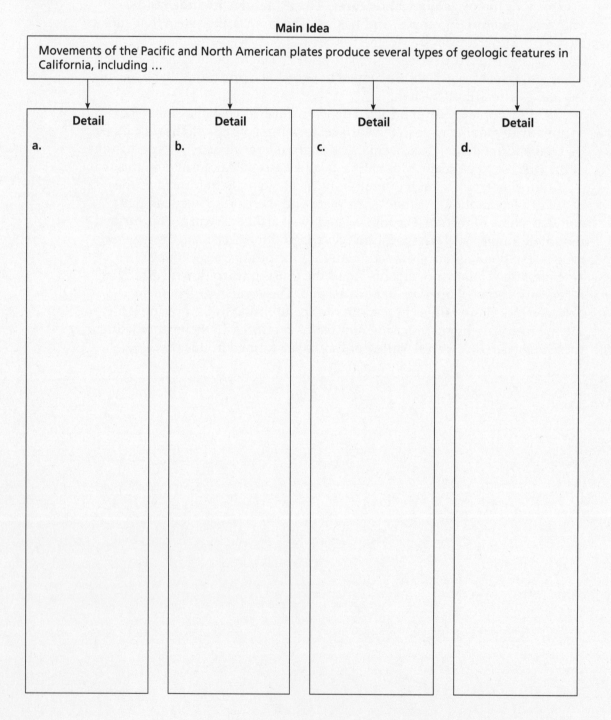

Main Idea

Movements of the Pacific and North American plates produce several types of geologic features in California, including …

Detail	Detail	Detail	Detail
a.	b.	c.	d.

Volcanoes ▪ *Reading/Notetaking Guide*

Plate Tectonics and California (pp. 235–237)

1. Is the following statement true or false? The movement of the North American plate and the Nazca plate produced California's major geological features.

   _____

2. What is the name of the fault that marks the boundary between the Pacific and North American plates?

   _____

3. Mount Shasta and Lassen Peak are volcanoes that formed as the result of what geologic process?

   a. fault movement
   b. mountain building
   c. subduction
   d. earthquakes

4. How is plate tectonic activity related to the formation of some of California's mountain ranges?

   _____

   _____

   _____

   _____

5. How did the Central Valley form?

   _____

   _____

   _____

   _____

6. The Central Valley is a

   a. mountain range.
   b. basin.
   c. volcano.
   d. plateau.

Volcanoes ▪ *Reading/Notetaking Guide*

California Geology *(continued)*

7. Identify the features labeled *a–d* on the map below.

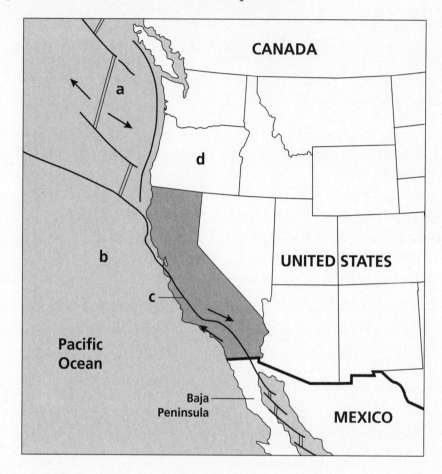

a. _____

b. _____

c. _____

d. _____

The Air Around You

Key Concepts

- What is the composition of Earth's atmosphere?
- How is the atmosphere important to living things?
- What causes smog and acid rain?

Weather is the condition of Earth's atmosphere at a particular time and place. Earth's **atmosphere** is the envelope of gases that surrounds the planet.

Earth's atmosphere is made up of nitrogen, oxygen, carbon dioxide, water vapor, and many other gases, as well as particles of liquids and solids.

Plants and animals take oxygen directly from air and use it to release energy from food. A form of oxygen called **ozone** contains three oxygen atoms in each molecule instead of the usual two.

Carbon dioxide is very important because plants need it to survive. The burning of fuels such as gasoline and coal also produces carbon dioxide. **Water vapor** is invisible—it is water in the form of a gas. Water vapor is important in weather. It produces clouds and precipitation.

Earth's atmosphere makes conditions on Earth suitable for living things. The atmosphere contains oxygen and other gases that living things need. The atmosphere also keeps Earth's surface warm and protects Earth from dangerous radiation and meteoroids.

Pollutants are harmful substances in the air, water, or soil. Air pollution can affect the health of humans and other living things. Some air pollution occurs naturally, but many types of pollution are the result of human activity. Although many natural processes add particles to the atmosphere, most air pollution is the result of burning fossil fuels, such as coal, oil, gasoline, and diesel fuels.

The burning of fossil fuels can cause smog and acid rain. The brown haze that develops in sunny cities is called photochemical smog. **Photochemical smog** is formed by the reaction of sunlight to pollutants such as hydrocarbons and nitrogen oxides.

Another result of air pollution is **acid rain,** rain that contains more acid than normal. Acid rain is sometimes strong enough to damage the surfaces of buildings and statues. It also harms lakes and ponds.

In the United States, federal and state governments have passed a number of laws and regulations to reduce air pollution. The Environmental Protection Agency (EPA) monitors the air pollutants in the United States. Air quality in this country has generally improved over the last 30 years. However, the air in many American cities is still polluted. There is an ongoing debate about the costs and benefits of stricter regulations.

The Atmosphere • *Reading/Notetaking Guide*

The Air Around You (pp. 256–261)

This section describes Earth's atmosphere, or the layer of gases that surrounds the planet. This section also describes harmful substances in the air, explains how they can affect people and things, and describes what has been done to improve air quality.

Use Target Reading Skills

Look at the illustration titled Gases in Dry Air on page 257 of your textbook. In the graphic organizer below, ask three questions that you have about the illustration. As you read about the composition of the atmosphere, write answers to your questions.

Composition of the Atmosphere

Q. What is the most common gas in the atmosphere?
A.
Q.
A.
Q.
A.

The Atmosphere ▪ *Reading/Notetaking Guide*

Introduction (p. 256)

1. The condition of Earth's atmosphere at a particular time and place is

   called _____.

2. What is Earth's atmosphere?

   _____

   _____

Composition of the Atmosphere (pp. 257–258)

3. Label the two larger pieces of the graph with the gases they represent.

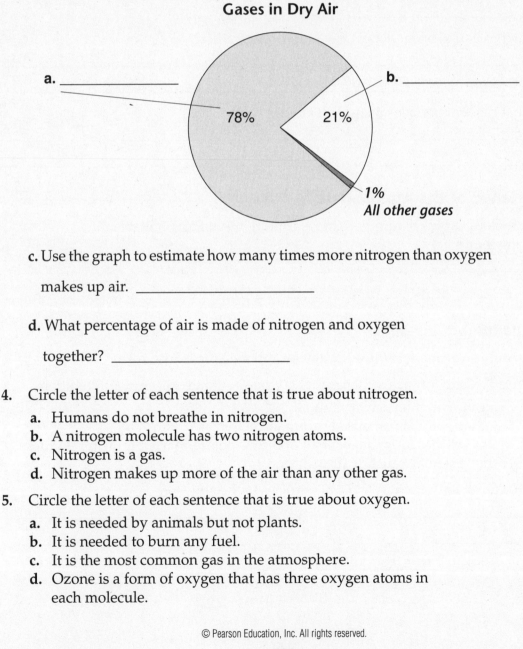

Gases in Dry Air

a. _____

b. _____

78%

21%

1%
All other gases

   c. Use the graph to estimate how many times more nitrogen than oxygen

   makes up air. _____

   d. What percentage of air is made of nitrogen and oxygen

   together? _____

4. Circle the letter of each sentence that is true about nitrogen.
   a. Humans do not breathe in nitrogen.
   b. A nitrogen molecule has two nitrogen atoms.
   c. Nitrogen is a gas.
   d. Nitrogen makes up more of the air than any other gas.

5. Circle the letter of each sentence that is true about oxygen.
   a. It is needed by animals but not plants.
   b. It is needed to burn any fuel.
   c. It is the most common gas in the atmosphere.
   d. Ozone is a form of oxygen that has three oxygen atoms in
      each molecule.

The Atmosphere ▪ *Reading/Notetaking Guide*

The Air Around You *(continued)*

6. Circle the letter of each sentence that is true about carbon dioxide.

    a. It is essential to life.

    b. It is given off by plants and animals as a waste product.

    c. It is used by animals to digest food.

    d. It is needed by fuels to burn.

7. Is the following sentence true or false? Carbon dioxide alone makes up almost 1 percent of dry air.

    _____

8. Water in the form of a gas is called _____.

9. Is the following sentence true or false? Water vapor is the same as steam.

    _____

10. What role does water vapor play in Earth's weather?

    _____

    _____

11. What types of particles does air contain?

    _____

    _____

Importance of the Atmosphere (p. 259)

12. How does Earth's atmosphere make conditions on Earth suitable for living things?

    _____

    _____

Air Quality (pp. 259–260)

13. Harmful substances in the air, water, or soil are known as _____.

14. Circle the letter of each sentence that is true about the causes of air pollution.

    a. Some air pollution occurs naturally.

    b. Some air pollution is caused by human activities.

    c. Motor vehicles cause almost half of the air pollution from human activities.

    d. Farming is not a cause of air pollution.

15. What are some natural sources of particles in the atmosphere?

    _____

    _____

    _____

The Atmosphere • *Reading/Notetaking Guide*

16. The brown haze that forms over sunny cities like Los Angeles is called

_____.

17. Circle the letter of each sentence that is true about photochemical smog.
   a. It is caused by the action of sunlight on chemicals in the air.
   b. It forms when particles in smoke combine with water droplets in air.
   c. It forms a mixture of ozone and other pollutants.
   d. It is harmless to living things.

18. What effects does smog have on people and things?

_____

_____

_____

19. Is the following sentence true or false? One result of air pollution is acid rain.

_____

20. Complete the flowchart to show causes, results, and effects related to acid rain.

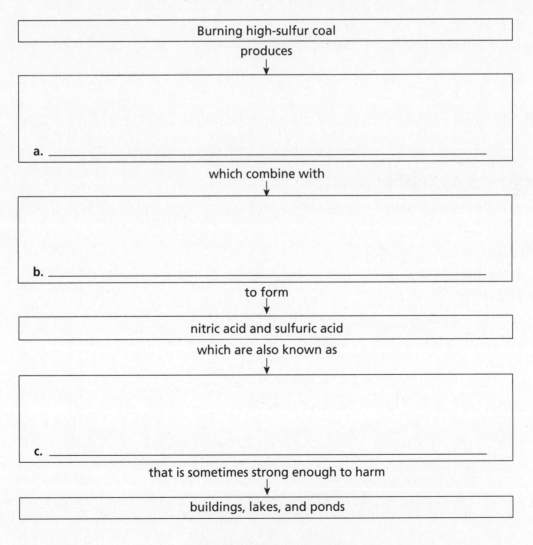

Burning high-sulfur coal

produces

a. _____

which combine with

b. _____

to form

nitric acid and sulfuric acid

which are also known as

c. _____

that is sometimes strong enough to harm

buildings, lakes, and ponds

The Atmosphere · *Reading/Notetaking Guide*

The Air Around You *(continued)*

    d. Identify the cause of sulfur oxides.

    _____

    e. How is sulfuric acid both a result and a cause?

    _____

    f. What is the end effect of burning high-sulfur coal?

    _____

21. Is the following sentence true or false? Rain is not naturally acidic.

_____

22. Rain that contains more acid than normal is known as

_____.

23. How can acid rain affect trees such as pines and spruce?

_____

_____

_____

_____

24. How can acid rain harm lakes and ponds?

_____

_____

_____

_____

Improving Air Quality (p. 261)

25. Is the following sentence true or false? Air quality in this country has generally worsened over the past 30 years.

_____

26. Is the following sentence true or false? The air in many American cities is still polluted.

_____

Chapter 7 The Atmosphere • *Section 2 Summary*

Air Pressure

Key Concepts

- What are some of the properties of air?

- What instruments are used to measure air pressure?

- How does increasing altitude affect air pressure and density?

Air consists of atoms and molecules that have mass. Therefore, air has mass. **Because air has mass, it also has other properties, including density and pressure.** The amount of mass in a given volume of air is its **density.** The force pushing on an area or surface is called **pressure. Air pressure** is the result of the weight of a column of air pushing down on an area. The molecules in air push in all directions. This is why air pressure doesn't crush objects.

A **barometer** is an instrument that is used to measure air pressure. **Two kinds of barometers are mercury barometers and aneroid barometers.** A **mercury barometer** consists of a glass tube open at the bottom end and partially filled with mercury. The open end of the tube rests in a dish of mercury, and the space above the mercury in the tube contains almost no air. The air pressure pushing down on the surface of the mercury in the dish is equal to the weight of the column of mercury in the tube. At sea level, the mercury column is about 76 centimeters high, on average. An **aneroid barometer** has an airtight metal chamber that is sensitive to changes in air pressure. The thin walls of the chamber flex in and out as air pressure changes, and the movements are recorded on a dial.

In weather reports, air pressure usually is given in inches of mercury. National Weather Service maps indicate air pressure in millibars. One inch of mercury equals 33.87 millibars.

Altitude, or elevation, is the distance above sea level. **Air pressure decreases as altitude increases. As air pressure decreases, so does density.** Sea-level air has the weight of the whole atmosphere pressing on it, so air pressure is higher at sea level. Air pressure is much lower at the tops of mountains. There, the low density of air can make it hard to breathe because there is less oxygen in each cubic meter of air.

The Atmosphere · *Reading/Notetaking Guide*

Air Pressure (pp. 262–266)

This section describes several properties of air, including density and air pressure. The section also explains how air pressure is measured and how it changes with altitude.

Use Target Reading Skills

Read the section "Properties of Air." Complete the notetaking graphic organizer below by filling in notes that correspond to the Recall Questions and by writing a summary of the section.

Recall Questions	Notes: Properties of Air
What properties does air have? What is density? What is pressure? What causes air pressure?	Air: has mass, density, and exerts pressure a. _____ _____ _____ Pressure: force exerted over an area b. _____ _____ _____

Section Summary: _____
_____
_____
_____

Introduction (p. 262)

1. Suppose that you are not carrying anything on your back. Why do your shoulders still have pressure on them?

   _____

   _____

Properties of Air (p. 263)

2. Circle the letter of each sentence that is true about air.

   a. Air has mass because it is composed of atoms and molecules.
   b. Because air has mass, it has density and pressure.
   c. The more molecules in a given volume of air, the greater its density.
   d. The greater the density of air, the less pressure it exerts.

3. Complete the cause-and-effect table to show the relationship among mass, volume, and density.

CAUSE		EFFECT
If mass	**and volume**	**then density**
increases	stays the same,	a.
b.	stays the same,	decreases.
stays the same	decreases,	c.
stays the same	d.	decreases.

e. Use the information in the table to write one or two sentences about the relationship among mass, volume, and density.

_____

_____

_____

_____

Measuring Air Pressure (pp. 264–265)

4. An instrument that is used to measure air pressure is a(n) _____.

5. What is the difference between how air pressure is indicated in a mercury barometer and an aneroid barometer?

_____

_____

_____

6. Draw a line on the glass tube to show where the level of the mercury might be if the air pressure fell.

← Mercury

Air pressure   Air pressure

The Atmosphere · *Reading/Notetaking Guide*

Air Pressure (continued)

7. Two different units used to measure air pressure are

   _____ and _____.

8. If the air pressure is 30 inches, how many millibars of air pressure are there?

   _____

   _____

Altitude and the Properties of Air (pp. 265–266)

9. Another word for elevation, or distance above sea level, is _____.

10. Is the following sentence true or false? Air pressure increases as altitude increases.

    _____

11. Is the following sentence true or false? As air pressure decreases, so does air density.

    _____

12. Why is air pressure greater at sea level than at the top of a mountain?

    _____

    _____

    _____

13. Is the following sentence true or false? As altitude increases, so does air density.

    _____

14. Explain why mountain climbers sometimes bring tanks of oxygen along with them on their climbs.

    _____

    _____

    _____

15. Circle the letter of the sentence that helps explain why you would have more difficulty breathing at high altitudes than at sea level.
    a. Air pressure is higher at high altitudes.
    b. Density of the air is greater at high altitudes.
    c. The percentage of oxygen in the air is lower at high altitudes.
    d. The amount of oxygen in each breath is less at high altitudes.

Layers of the Atmosphere

Key Concepts

- What are the four main layers of the atmosphere?

- What are the characteristics of each layer?

As you rise up through the atmosphere, air pressure and temperature change dramatically. **Scientists divide Earth's atmosphere into four main layers classified according to changes in temperature. These layers are the troposphere, the stratosphere, the mesosphere, and the thermosphere.**

You live in the inner, or lowest layer of Earth's atmosphere, the **troposphere. The troposphere is the layer of the atmosphere in which Earth's weather occurs.** The depth of the troposphere varies from 16 kilometers above the equator to less than 9 kilometers above the North and South Poles.

The **stratosphere** extends from the top of the troposphere to about 50 kilometers above Earth's surface. **The stratosphere is the second layer of the atmosphere and contains the ozone layer.** The ozone layer is important because it protects Earth's living things from dangerous ultraviolet radiation from the sun.

Above the stratosphere, a drop in temperature marks the beginning of the next layer, the **mesosphere.** The mesosphere begins 50 kilometers above Earth's surface and ends at an altitude of 80 kilometers. **The mesosphere is the layer of the atmosphere that protects Earth's surface from being hit by most meteoroids.**

The outmost layer of Earth's atmosphere is the thermosphere. The **thermosphere** extends from 80 kilometers above Earth's surface outward into space. It has no definite outer limit, but blends gradually with outer space. The air in the thermosphere is very hot, up to 1,800°C. Despite the high temperature, you would not feel warm in the thermosphere. **Temperature** is the average amount of energy of motion of all the particles of a substance. Because there are so few particles in the thermosphere, an ordinary thermometer cannot accurately measure the temperature there.

The thermosphere is divided into two layers. The lower layer, called the **ionosphere,** begins about 80 kilometers above the surface and extends to about 400 kilometers. Gas molecules here are electrically charged because of the sun's energy. Radio waves bounce back from the ionosphere to Earth's surface. The brilliant light displays called auroras also occur in the ionosphere. The outer layer of the thermosphere is the **exosphere.**

The Atmosphere · *Reading/Notetaking Guide*

Layers of the Atmosphere (pp. 267–271)

This section describes the four main layers of the atmosphere.

Use Target Reading Skills

As you preview Figure 12 in your textbook, write questions in the appropriate spaces in the graphic organizer. As you read, fill in the answers under the questions.

Layers of the Atmosphere

Q. Where is the ozone layer?
A.
Q.
A.

Introduction (p. 267)

1. The four main layers of the atmosphere are classified according to

   changes in _____.

The Troposphere (p. 268)

2. Circle the letter of each sentence that is true about the troposphere.
   a. It is the lowest layer of Earth's atmosphere.
   b. It has less variable conditions than other layers.
   c. It is where Earth's weather occurs.
   d. It is the shallowest layer of the atmosphere.

3. Is the following sentence true or false? The troposphere contains almost all of the mass of the atmosphere.

   _____

4. Is the following sentence true or false? As altitude increases in the troposphere, temperature also increases.

   _____

The Atmosphere ▪ *Reading/Notetaking Guide*

5. How does the depth of the troposphere vary?

   _____

   _____

   _____

   _____

   _____

6. Is the following sentence true or false? At the top of the troposphere, the temperature stops decreasing.

   _____

The Stratosphere (pp. 268–269)

7. How far does the stratosphere extend above Earth's surface?

   _____

   _____

8. Circle the letter of each sentence that is true about the stratosphere.
   a. The temperature of the lower stratosphere is about −60°C.
   b. The upper stratosphere is colder than the lower stratosphere.
   c. The middle portion of the stratosphere contains a layer of ozone.
   d. The ozone in the stratosphere reflects energy from the sun.

The Mesosphere (p. 270)

9. Where does the mesosphere begin?

   _____

   _____

10. Circle the letter of each sentence that is true about the mesosphere.
    a. It contains the ozone layer.
    b. Temperatures approach −90°C in the outer mesosphere.
    c. It protects Earth's surface from being hit by most meteoroids.
    d. It ends at 320 kilometers above sea level.

The Atmosphere • *Reading/Notetaking Guide*

Layers of the Atmosphere *(continued)*

The Thermosphere (pp. 270–271)

11. Circle the letter of each sentence that is true about the thermosphere.
    a. It is the outermost layer of the atmosphere.
    b. Its air is very thin.
    c. It has no definite outer limit.
    d. It starts at 320 kilometers above sea level.

12. Why is the thermosphere so hot?

    _____

    _____

    _____

    _____

    _____

13. Why would an ordinary thermometer show a low temperature in the thermosphere?

    _____

    _____

    _____

    _____

14. List the layers of the thermosphere, and describe where each begins above Earth's surface.

    a. _____

    b. _____

15. Brilliant light displays that occur in the ionosphere are called

    _____.

Chapter 7 The Atmosphere • *Section 4 Summary*

Energy in Earth's Atmosphere

Key Concepts

■ In what form does energy from the sun travel to Earth?

■ What happens to the sun's energy when it reaches Earth?

Nearly all of the energy in Earth's atmosphere comes from the sun. This energy travels to Earth as **electromagnetic waves,** a form of energy that can travel through space. Electromagnetic waves are classified according to wavelength, or distance between waves. The direct transfer of energy by electromagnetic waves is called **radiation.**

Most of the energy from the sun travels to Earth in the form of visible light. However, a full spectrum of electromagnetic energy is present in solar radiation. Visible light is a mixture of all of the colors that you see in a rainbow. The different colors are the result of different wavelengths of visible light. Red and orange light have the longest wavelengths, and blue and violet have the shortest wavelengths.

Infrared radiation is a form of energy with wavelengths that are longer than those of red light. Infrared radiation is not visible, but can be felt as heat. **Ultraviolet radiation** is a form of energy with wavelengths that are shorter than those of violet light. Ultraviolet radiation can cause sunburns, skin cancer, and eye damage.

Some sunlight is absorbed or reflected by the atmosphere before it can reach the surface. The rest passes through the atmosphere to the surface. Dust particles and gases in the atmosphere reflect light from the sun in all directions. This is called **scattering.** Scattered light looks bluer than ordinary sunlight, which is why the daytime sky looks blue. During sunrise and sunset, when sunlight passes through a greater thickness of atmosphere, scattering removes more blue light and causes the sun to look red.

When Earth's surface is heated, it radiates most of the energy back into the atmosphere as infrared radiation. Much of this longer-wavelength radiation cannot travel all the way through the atmosphere back into space. Instead, much of it is absorbed by water vapor, carbon dioxide, and other gases in the air. The process by which gases hold heat in the air is called the **greenhouse effect.** The greenhouse effect is a natural process that keeps Earth's atmosphere at a temperature that is comfortable for most living things. However, emissions from human activities may be altering this process.

The Atmosphere • *Reading/Notetaking Guide*

Energy in Earth's Atmosphere (pp. 272–275)

This section explains how the atmosphere, or the air around Earth, is heated.

Use Target Reading Skills

Read the section "Energy in the Atmosphere." Complete the notetaking graphic organizer below by filling in notes that correspond to the Recall Questions and by writing a summary of the section.

Recall Questions	Notes: Energy in the Atmosphere
What happens to the sun's energy when it reaches Earth's atmosphere?	Incoming sunlight: partially absorbed, partially reflected, rest reaches Earth's surface
What in the atmosphere absorbs energy?	a. _____ _____ _____
How does the atmosphere reflect energy?	b. _____ _____ _____

Section Summary: _____
_____
_____

Energy From the Sun (pp. 272–273)

1. Is the following sentence true or false? Nearly half of the energy in Earth's atmosphere comes from the sun. _____

2. Energy from the sun travels to Earth as _____.

3. Is the following sentence true or false? Electromagnetic waves are classified according to wavelength, or the distance between waves.

   _____

4. The direct transfer of energy by electromagnetic waves is called _____.

Match the type of radiation with its description.

Type of Radiation

_____ 5. visible light

_____ 6. infrared radiation

_____ 7. ultraviolet radiation

Description

a. It is a mixture of all of the colors of the rainbow.

b. It has wavelengths that are shorter than those of violet light.

c. It has wavelengths that are longer than those of red light.

The Atmosphere ▪ *Reading/Notetaking Guide*

8. What causes the different colors of visible light?

_____

_____

_____

9. Is the following sentence true or false? Red light has a shorter wavelength than blue light.

_____

10. Circle the letter of each sentence that is true about infrared radiation.

   a. It is invisible.
   b. It can be felt as heat.
   c. It has longer wavelengths than red light has.
   d. It causes sunburn.

11. Circle the letter of each sentence that is true about ultraviolet radiation.

   a. It makes up most of the energy from the sun that reaches Earth.
   b. It can cause skin cancer and eye damage.
   c. It has longer wavelengths than violet light has.
   d. It can cause sunburn.

Energy in the Atmosphere (p. 274)

12. What happens to energy from the sun that is neither reflected nor absorbed by the atmosphere?

_____

_____

13. What absorbs energy from the sun in the atmosphere?

_____

_____

_____

14. What reflects energy from the sun in the atmosphere?

_____

_____

15. Reflection of light in all directions is called _____.

16. Circle the letter of each sentence that is true about scattering.

   a. Short wavelengths of visible light scatter less than long wavelengths.
   b. Blue light scatters less than red light.
   c. Scattered light is bluer than ordinary sunlight.
   d. Scattering explains why the daytime sky looks blue.

The Atmosphere • *Reading/Notetaking Guide*

Energy in Earth's Atmosphere *(continued)*

Energy at Earth's Surface *(p. 275)*

17. Energy that is absorbed by the land and water is changed into

_____ .

18. Is the following sentence true or false? When Earth's surface is heated, it radiates most of the energy back into the atmosphere as ultraviolet radiation.

_____

19. What absorbs most of the energy that is radiated from Earth's surface?

_____

_____

_____

20. The process by which gases hold heat in the air is called the

_____ .

21. Is the following sentence true or false? The greenhouse effect is a natural process.

_____

Chapter 7 The Atmosphere · *Section 5 Summary*

Heat Transfer in the Atmosphere

Key Concepts

- How is temperature measured?
- In what three ways is heat transferred?
- How is heat transferred in the troposphere?

All substances are made up of small particles, which can be atoms or molecules, that are constantly moving. The faster the molecules are moving, the more energy they have. The total energy of motion in the particles of a substance is called **thermal energy.** Temperature is the average amount of energy of motion in each particle of a substance. It is a measure of how hot or cold a substance is. Temperature is one of the most important factors affecting the weather.

Air temperature is usually measured with a thermometer. A **thermometer** is a thin glass tube with a bulb on one end that contains a liquid, usually colored alcohol. Thermometers work because liquids expand when they are heated and contract when they are cooled.

Temperature is measured in units called degrees. On the Celsius scale, the freezing point of pure water is 0°C and the boiling point of pure water is 100°C. On the Fahrenheit scale, the freezing point of water is 32°F and the boiling point is 212°F.

Heat is the transfer of thermal energy from a hotter object to a cooler one. **Heat is transferred in three ways within the atmosphere: radiation, conduction, and convection.** Radiation is the direct transfer of energy by electromagnetic waves. The direct transfer of heat from one substance to another substance that it is touching is called **conduction.** Conduction works well in some solids, but not as well in fluids (liquids and gases). In fluids, molecules can move from place to place and take their heat with them. The transfer of heat by the movement of a fluid is called **convection.**

Radiation, conduction, and convection work together to heat the troposphere. Air near Earth's surface is warmed by conduction of heat from the surface to the air. **Within the troposphere, heat is transferred mostly by convection.** When the air near the ground is heated, the molecules have more energy and move faster. The molecules bump into one another and move farther apart, and the air becomes less dense. Cooler, denser air sinks, forcing the warmer, less dense air to rise. The upward movement of warm air and the downward movement of cool air form **convection currents.** Convection currents move heat thoughout the troposphere.

The Atmosphere ▪ *Reading/Notetaking Guide*

Heat Transfer in the Atmosphere (pp. 278–281)

This section explains what temperature measures and how temperature is related to heat. The section also describes three ways by which heat can be transferred from a hotter object to a cooler one.

Use Target Reading Skills

As you read about heat transfer, complete the outline to show the relationship among the headings.

Heat Transfer

I. Thermal Energy and Temperature

    A. _____

    B. _____

II. _____

    A. _____

    B. _____

    C. _____

    D. _____

Thermal Energy and Temperature (p. 279)

1. Is the following sentence true or false? The faster the particles of a substance are moving, the more energy they have.

_____

2. The total energy of motion in the particles of a substance is called

_____.

3. The average amount of energy of motion of each particle of a substance

is called _____.

4. Air temperature is usually measured with a(n) _____.

5. How does a thermometer work?

_____

_____

_____

_____

The Atmosphere · *Reading/Notetaking Guide*

6. Complete the compare/contrast table to show the difference between the two temperature scales.

Temperature Scales		
Scale	**Freezing Point of Water**	**Boiling Point of Water**
Celsius	a.	b.
Fahrenheit	c.	d.

    e. Is 50° hotter on a Celsius or on a Fahrenheit scale? Explain your answer by comparing the numbers in the table.

_____

_____

_____

How Heat Is Transferred (pp. 280–281)

7. The energy transferred from a hotter object to a cooler one is referred to

as _____.

8. Is the following sentence true or false? Radiation is the direct transfer of energy by electromagnetic waves.

_____

9. The direct transfer of heat from one substance to another substance that

it is touching is called _____.

10. Circle the letter of each sentence that is true about conduction.
    a. It works well in some solids.
    b. It works well in metals.
    c. It works best in liquids.
    d. It works very well in air.

11. The transfer of heat by the movement of a fluid is called

_____.

Match the type of heat transfer with its example.

Heat Transfer	**Example**
____ **12.** radiation	**a.** warm water rising in a pot on a stove
____ **13.** conduction	**b.** burning your bare feet on hot sand
____ **14.** convection	**c.** feeling the sun's warmth on your face

The Atmosphere ▪ *Reading/Notetaking Guide*

Heat Transfer in the Atmosphere (continued)

15. In the drawing, label each of the ways by which heat is transferred in the troposphere.

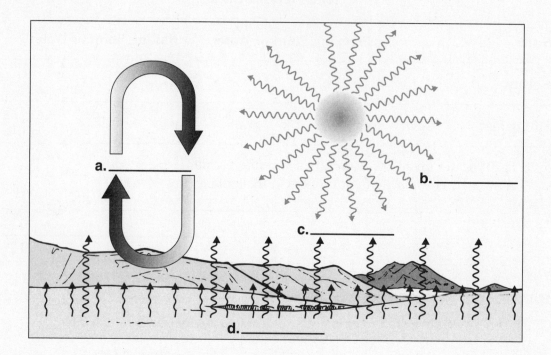

a. _____

b. _____

c. _____

d. _____

16. The troposphere is heated mainly by _____.

17. The upward movement of warm air and the downward movement of cool air form _____.

Chapter 7 The Atmosphere ▪ *Section 6 Summary*

Winds

Key Concepts

- What causes winds?
- How do local winds and global winds differ?
- Where are the major global wind belts located?

A **wind** is the horizontal movement of air from an area of high pressure to an area of lower pressure. **Winds are caused by differences in air pressure.** Most differences in air pressure are caused by unequal heating of the atmosphere. Convection currents form when Earth's surface is heated by the sun. Cool, dense air with higher air pressure flows underneath warm, less dense air, forcing the warm air to rise.

Winds are described by their direction and speed. Wind direction is determined with a wind vane. The name of a wind tells you the direction the wind is coming from. Wind speed is measured with an **anemometer.**

Wind blowing over your skin removes body heat. The increased cooling that a wind can cause is called the **wind-chill factor.**

Local winds are winds that blow over short distances. **Local winds are caused by the unequal heating of Earth's surface within a small area.** Local winds form only when large-scale winds are weak.

A **sea breeze** is a local wind that blows from an ocean or a lake. The sun heats land faster than it heats water, so during the day the air over land becomes warmer than the air over water. The cool air blows inland from the water and moves underneath the warm air. At night, land cools more quickly than water, so air over land becomes cooler than air over water. The cool air blows toward the water from the land and moves underneath the warm air. The flow of air from land to a body of water is called a **land breeze.**

Winds that blow steadily from specific directions over long distances are called **global winds. Like local winds, global winds are created by the unequal heating of Earth's surface. But unlike local winds, global winds occur over a large area.** Because Earth is rotating, global winds do not follow a straight path. The way Earth's rotation makes winds curve is called the **Coriolis effect.** In the Northern Hemisphere, global winds curve to the right. In the Southern Hemisphere, global winds curve to the left.

The Coriolis effect and other factors combine to produce a pattern of calm areas and wind belts around Earth. **The major global wind belts are the trade winds, the polar easterlies, and the prevailing westerlies.** The calm areas are called the doldrums and horse latitudes. **Latitude** is distance from the equator, measured in degrees. The trade winds blow between the equator and 30° north and south latitude, the prevailing westerlies between 30° and 60° north and south latitude, and the polar easterlies between 60° north and south latitude and the poles.

About 10 kilometers above Earth's surface are bands of high-speed winds called **jet streams.** These generally blow from west to east.

The Atmosphere · *Reading/Notetaking Guide*

Winds (pp. 282–288)

This section explains what causes winds and how winds are measured. The section also describes different types of winds that blow across Earth's surface.

Use Target Reading Skills

Read the section "Local Winds." Complete the notetaking graphic organizer below by filling in notes that correspond to the Recall Questions and by writing a summary of the section.

Recall Questions	Notes: Local Winds
What is a local wind?	Local wind: wind that blows a short distance
What is a sea breeze?	a. _____ _____ _____
What is a land breeze?	b. _____ _____ _____
Section Summary: _____ _____ _____	

What Is Wind? (p. 283)

1. The horizontal movement of air from an area of high pressure to an area of lower pressure is referred to as _____.

2. Is the following sentence true or false? Winds are caused by differences in air pressure. _____

Match the instrument with what it measures.

Instrument	What It Measures
____ 3. wind vane	a. wind speed
____ 4. anemometer	b. wind direction

5. Is the following sentence true or false? A south wind blows toward the south.

   _____

6. The increased cooling that a wind can cause is called the _____.

7. Why does the wind blowing over your skin make you feel colder?

_____

_____

Local Winds (p. 284)

8. Winds that blow over short distances are called _____.

9. What causes local winds?

_____

_____

10. Circle the letter of each sentence that is true about the unequal heating of land and water.

    a. Land warms up faster than water.
    b. During the day, air over water is warmer than air over land.
    c. Water cools more quickly than land.
    d. At night, air over water is cooler than air over land.

11. Label the drawings to indicate which drawing shows a sea breeze and which drawing shows a land breeze.

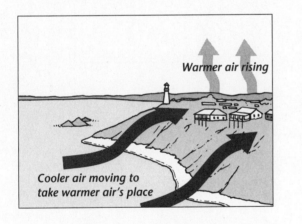

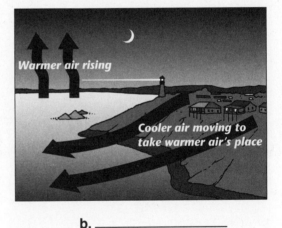

a. _____

b. _____

Global Winds (p. 285)

12. Winds that blow steadily from specific directions over long distances are

    called _____.

13. Circle the letter of each sentence that is true about global winds.

    a. They are created by unequal heating of Earth's surface.
    b. They are produced by the movement of air between the equator and the poles.
    c. They blow in a straight line from the poles toward the equator.
    d. They curve because of Earth's rotation.

The Atmosphere · *Reading/Notetaking Guide*

Winds *(continued)*

14. As Earth rotates, the Coriolis effect causes winds in the Northern

Hemisphere to turn toward the _____.

Global Wind Belts (pp. 286–288)

15. The calm areas around Earth include the _____

and the _____.

16. Complete the compare/contrast table to show the differences among the
major wind belts.

Direction of Global Wind Belts	
Wind Belt	**Direction It Blows**
Trade winds	**a.**
Prevailing westerlies	**b.**
Polar easterlies	**c.**

d. Suppose you were sailing from Central America to Asia just above
the equator. Which winds would help speed you on your way?

_____

17. Circle the letter of each sentence that is true about jet streams.

a. They are about 100 kilometers above Earth's surface.
b. They are hundreds of kilometers wide.
c. They blow from east to west.
d. They blow at speeds of 200 to 400 kilometers per hour.

Chapter 8 Weather • *Section 1 Summary*

Water in the Atmosphere

Key Concepts

- What is humidity and how is it measured?
- How do clouds form?
- What are the three main types of clouds?

Water is constantly moving between Earth's surface and the atmosphere in the **water cycle.** Water vapor enters the air by evaporation from the oceans and other bodies of water. **Evaporation** is the process by which water molecules in liquid water escape into the air as water vapor. Some of the water vapor in the atmosphere condenses to form clouds. Then rain and other forms of precipitation fall from the clouds toward Earth's surface.

Humidity is a measure of the amount of water vapor in the air. The percentage of water vapor that is actually in the air compared to the amount of water vapor the air can hold at a particular temperature is called the **relative humidity. Relative humidity can be measured with an instrument called a psychrometer. A psychrometer** has two thermometers, a wet-bulb thermometer and a dry-bulb thermometer. Air is blown over both thermometers. Because the wet-bulb thermometer is cooled by evaporation, its reading drops below that of the dry-bulb thermometer. The relative humidity can be found by comparing the temperatures of the wet-bulb and dry-bulb thermometers.

Clouds form when water vapor in the air condenses to form liquid water or ice crystals. The process by which molecules of water vapor in the air become liquid water is called **condensation.** As air cools, the amount of water vapor it can hold decreases. When the air becomes saturated, some of the water vapor in the air condenses into water or ice. The temperature at which condensation begins is called the **dew point.** If the dew point is below the freezing point, the water vapor may change directly into ice crystals. For water vapor to condense, tiny particles must be present so that the water has a surface on which to condense. Water that condenses from the air onto a cold surface, such as blades of grass, is called dew. Frost is ice that has been deposited on a surface whose temperature is below freezing.

Scientists classify clouds into three main types based on their shape: cirrus, cumulus, and stratus. Clouds are further classified by their altitude. Wispy, feathery clouds are called **cirrus** clouds. Cirrus clouds form only at high levels, and they are made of ice crystals. Clouds that look like fluffy, rounded piles of cotton are called **cumulus** clouds. Cumulus clouds usually indicate fair weather. Towering cumulus clouds with flat tops, called cumulonimbus clouds, often produce thunderstorms. Clouds that form in flat layers are called **stratus** clouds. Stratus clouds that produce rain or snow are called nimbostratus clouds. Clouds that form at or near the ground are called fog. Altocumulus and altostratus clouds are middle-level clouds that form 2–6 kilometers above Earth's surface. Fog often forms when the ground cools at night after a warm, humid day.

Weather ▪ *Reading/Notetaking Guide*

Water in the Atmosphere (pp. 300–306)

This section explains what humidity is and how it is measured. The section also explains how clouds form and describes different types of clouds.

Use Target Reading Skills

Complete the first column in the chart by filling in the red headings. Then in the second column, ask a what, how, *or* where *question for each heading. As you read the section, complete the third column with the answers.*

Section 1: Water in the Atmosphere		
Heading	**Question**	**Answer**

Introduction (p. 300)

1. What is the water cycle?

    _____

    _____

2. The process by which water molecules in liquid water escape into the air as water vapor is called _____.

Weather ▪ *Reading/Notetaking Guide*

Humidity (pp. 301–302)

3.   A measure of the amount of water vapor in the air is _____.

4.   What is relative humidity?

_____

_____

_____

5.   Circle the letter of each sentence that is true about relative humidity.

   a. It is a percentage.
   b. It is all the water vapor that the air can hold.
   c. It depends on air temperature.
   d. It measures how windy it is.

6.   Relative humidity can be measured with a(n) _____.

7.   Circle the letter of each sentence that is true about how a psychrometer works.

   a. The dry-bulb thermometer is cooled by evaporation when the wind blows.
   b. The higher the humidity, the faster water evaporates from the bulb.
   c. The wet-bulb thermometer reading is always higher than the dry-bulb reading.
   d. When relative humidity is high, there is not much difference between the wet-bulb and dry-bulb thermometer readings.

How Clouds Form (p. 303)

8.   Is the following sentence true or false? Clouds form when water vapor in the air condenses to form liquid water or ice crystals.

   _____

Match the term with its definition.

	Term	Definition
____	**9.** condensation	**a.** Ice that has been deposited on a surface with a temperature that is below freezing
____	**10.** dew point	**b.** Water that condenses from the air onto a cooler surface
____	**11.** dew	**c.** Temperature at which condensation begins
____	**12.** frost	**d.** Process by which molecules of water vapor become liquid water

Weather • *Reading/Notetaking Guide*

Water in the Atmosphere *(continued)*

13. Circle the letter of each sentence that is true about condensation of water vapor.

   a. It occurs when air gets warmer.
   b. It can occur on cold surfaces.
   c. It explains why clouds form.
   d. It can form on dust particles.

Types of Clouds (pp. 304–306)

Match the type of cloud with the type of weather it is generally associated with.

Type of Cloud	Type of Weather
____ **14.** cumulus	**a.** Fair
____ **15.** nimbostratus	**b.** Storm on the way
____ **16.** cirrocumulus	**c.** Thunderstorms
____ **17.** cumulonimbus	**d.** Drizzle, rain, or snow

18. Circle the letter of each sentence that is true about cloud types.

   a. Cumulus clouds are usually a sign that a storm is approaching.
   b. Cumulonimbus and nimbostratus clouds produce rain or snow.
   c. Altostratus clouds are lower than regular stratus clouds.
   d. Cirrus clouds are made up of ice crystals.

Chapter 8 Weather · *Section 2 Summary*

Precipitation

Key Concept

- What are the common types of precipitation?

Precipitation is any form of water that falls from clouds and reaches Earth's surface. For precipitation to occur, cloud droplets or ice crystals must grow heavy enough to fall through the air. One way that cloud droplets grow is by colliding and combining with other cloud droplets. When the droplets become heavy enough, they fall out of the cloud as raindrops.

Common types of precipitation include rain, hail, snow, sleet, and freezing rain. The most common kind of precipitation is rain. Drops of water are called rain if they are at least 0.5 millimeter in diameter. Precipitation made up of smaller drops of water is called mist or drizzle. Round pellets of ice larger than 5 millimeters in diameter are called hailstones.

Hail forms only inside cumulonimbus clouds during thunderstorms. Strong updrafts in the cloud carry the hailstone up and down through the cold region many times, each time adding a new layer of ice to the hailstone. Eventually, the hailstone becomes heavy enough to fall to the ground.

Snow forms when water vapor in a cloud is converted directly into ice crystals called snowflakes. Each snowflake has six sides or branches. Dry air produces powdery snow. Humid air produces wet clumps of snow.

Sleet forms when raindrops fall through a layer of freezing air and turn into solid ice particles. Ice particles smaller than 5 millimeters in diameter are called sleet.

Freezing rain forms when raindrops freeze on a cold surface. As the rain continues to freeze on surfaces, a thick layer of ice may build up, which can break tree branches and power lines.

Weather · *Reading/Notetaking Guide*

Precipitation (pp. 307–309)

This section explains how rain, snow, and other common types of precipitation occur.

Use Target Reading Skills

As you read about the five types of precipitation, complete the compare-and-contrast table below.

Type	Appearance	How Forms
a.	Liquid water droplets	Water droplets in clouds collide and grow heavy enough to fall
Hail	b.	c.
d.	e.	Water vapor in clouds converted directly into ice crystals
Sleet	Small ice particles	f.
g.	Liquid in air turns to ice on ground	h.

Introduction (p. 307)

1. What is precipitation?

   _____

   _____

   _____

2. Is the following sentence true or false? All clouds produce precipitation.

   _____

3. Complete the flowchart to describe how clouds produce precipitation.

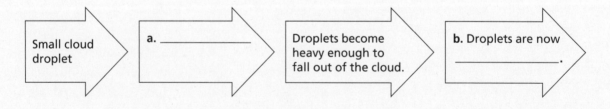

Small cloud droplet

a. _____

Droplets become heavy enough to fall out of the cloud.

b. Droplets are now _____.

Weather · *Reading/Notetaking Guide*

Types of Precipitation

4. Complete the table that compares three types of precipitation.

Type of Precipitation	Description and Size
Rain	a.
Hail	b.
Sleet	c.

d. How are rain, hail, and sleet similar and how are they different?

_____

_____

_____

_____

e. How does the humidity of air affect the type of snow that falls?

_____

_____

5. Is the following sentence true or false? The most common kind of precipitation is snow.

_____

6. How do mist and drizzle differ from rain?

_____

_____

_____

Weather • *Reading/Notetaking Guide*

Precipitation *(continued)*

7. How can freezing rain cause power failures?

_____

_____

_____

Match the type of precipitation with how it forms.

Precipitation		How It Forms

_____ **8.** sleet

_____ **9.** freezing rain

_____ **10.** hail

_____ **11.** snow

a. Water vapor in a cloud is converted directly into ice crystals.

b. Ice pellets add layers of ice as they are carried up and down in a cumulonimbus cloud.

c. Raindrops freeze after they hit the ground or other cold surfaces.

d. Raindrops freeze into tiny particles of ice as they fall through the air.

12. What damage can large hailstones do?

_____

_____

_____

Air Masses and Fronts

Key Concepts

- What are the major types of air masses in North America, and how do they move?

- What are the main types of fronts?

- What type of weather is associated with cyclones and anticyclones?

A huge body of air that has similar temperature, humidity, and air pressure at any given height is called an **air mass.** Scientists classify air masses according to temperature and humidity. **Four major types of air masses influence the weather in North America: maritime tropical, continental tropical, maritime polar, and continental polar. Tropical,** or warm, air masses form in the tropics and have low air pressure. **Polar,** or cold, air masses form north of 50° north latitude and south of 50° south latitude and have high air pressure. **Maritime** air masses form over oceans and are humid. **Continental** air masses form over land and are dry.

Maritime tropical air masses from the Pacific Ocean bring warm, humid air to the West Coast. Maritime polar air masses from the Pacific Ocean bring cool, humid air to the West Coast. Continental tropical air masses from the Southwest bring hot, dry air to the southern Great Plains. Continental polar air masses from central and northern Canada bring cold air to the central and eastern United States.

In the continental United States, air masses are commonly moved by the prevailing westerlies and jet streams. The prevailing westerlies generally push air masses from west to east in the United States. As air masses move across the land and the oceans, they collide with each other. However, if they have different temperatures and densities, they do not mix. The boundary where the air masses meet becomes a **front.** When air masses meet at a front, the collision often causes storms and changeable weather.

Colliding air masses can form four types of fronts: cold fronts, warm fronts, stationary fronts, and occluded fronts. A cold front forms when cold air moves underneath warm air, forcing the warm air to rise. Cold fronts move quickly and bring cold, dry air. A warm front forms when warm air moves over cold air. Warm fronts move slowly and bring warm, humid air. A stationary front forms when cold and warm air masses meet but neither one has enough force to move the other. It may bring many days of clouds and precipitation. An occluded front forms when a warm air mass is caught between two cooler air masses. The warm air mass is cut off, or **occluded,** from the ground. The occluded warm front may cause clouds and precipitation.

A swirling center of low air pressure is called a **cyclone.** Cyclones are also called "lows." **Cyclones and decreasing air pressure are associated with clouds, winds, and precipitation. Anticyclones** are high-pressure centers. They are also called "highs." **The descending air in an anticyclone generally causes dry, clear weather.** Because of the Coriolis effect, in the Northern Hemisphere winds spin in a counterclockwise direction in a cyclone and in a clockwise direction in an anticyclone.

Weather · *Reading/Notetaking Guide*

Air Masses and Fronts (pp. 310–317)

This section describes huge bodies of air, called air masses, and explains how they move. The section also explains how the meeting of different air masses affects weather.

Use Target Reading Skills

As you read about the four types of fronts, complete the compare-and-contrast table below.

Front	How It Forms	Type of Weather
Cold front	A cold air mass overtakes a warm air mass.	a.
Warm front	b.	c.
Occluded front	d.	e.
Stationary front	f.	g.

Introduction (p. 310)

1. What is an air mass?

   _____

   _____

   _____

Types of Air Masses (pp. 311–312)

2. Scientists classify air masses according to _____
   and _____.

3. Is the following sentence true or false? Polar air masses have low air pressure.

   _____

Weather · *Reading/Notetaking Guide*

4. Complete the compare/contrast table that shows the types of air masses and their characteristics.

Type of Air Mass	Characteristics
a.	Warm and humid
b.	Cool and humid
c.	Warm and dry
d.	Cold and dry

   e. How are maritime tropical and marine polar air masses alike, and how are they different?

   _____

   _____

   f. How are continental tropical and continental polar air masses alike, and how are they different?

   _____

   _____

How Air Masses Move (p. 313)

5. In the continental United States, major wind belts generally push air masses from _____ to _____.

6. How do jet streams affect air masses?

   _____

   _____

Types of Fronts (pp. 314–315)

7. Label the drawings to indicate a cold front and a warm front.

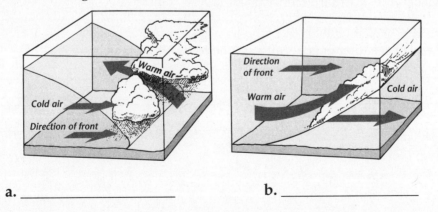

   a. _____   **b.** _____

Weather • *Reading/Notetaking Guide*

Air Masses and Fronts (continued)

Match the type of front with how it forms.

Type of Front

_____ 8. cold front

_____ 9. warm front

_____ 10. stationary front

_____ 11. occluded front

How It Forms

a. A fast-moving warm air mass overtakes a slowly moving cold air mass.

b. A warm air mass is caught between two cooler air masses.

c. A rapidly moving cold air mass runs into a slowly moving warm air mass.

d. A cold air mass and a warm air mass meet and remain stalled over an area.

12. Circle the letter of each sentence that is true about fronts.

a. Cold fronts can bring violent thunderstorms.
b. Warm fronts are associated with clouds and rain.
c. Stationary fronts may bring many days of clouds and precipitation.
d. Occluded fronts always bring fair weather.

Cyclones and Anticyclones (pp. 316–317)

13. A swirling center of low air pressure is called a(n) _____.

14. Is the following sentence true or false? Winds spiral inward toward the center of a cyclone.

_____

15. What type of weather is associated with cyclones?

_____

_____

_____

16. Is the following sentence true or false? Winds in an anticyclone spin clockwise in the Northern Hemisphere.

_____

17. What type of weather is generally associated with anticyclones?

_____

_____

_____

Storms

Key Concepts

- What are the main kinds of storms, and how do they form?
- What measures can you take to ensure safety in a storm?

A **storm** is a violent disturbance in the atmosphere. A **thunderstorm** is a small storm often accompanied by heavy precipitation and frequent thunder and lightning. **Thunderstorms form in large cumulonimbus clouds, also known as thunderheads.** During a thunderstorm, areas of positive and negative electrical charges build up in the storm clouds. **Lightning** is a sudden spark, or electrical discharge, between parts of a cloud, between nearby clouds, or between a cloud and the ground. A lightning bolt heats the air near it, and the rapidly heated air expands suddenly and explosively. Thunder is the sound of the explosion. Because light travels faster than sound, you see lightning before you hear thunder. **During thunderstorms, avoid places where lightning may strike. Also avoid objects that can conduct electricity, such as metal objects and bodies of water.**

A **tornado** is a rapidly whirling, funnel-shaped cloud that reaches down from a storm cloud to touch Earth's surface. **Tornadoes most commonly develop in thick cumulonimbus clouds—the same clouds that bring thunderstorms.** Tornadoes occur most often in the Great Plains, but they can and do occur in nearly every part of the United States. If you hear a tornado warning, move to a safe area as soon as you can. **The safest place to be during a tornado is in a storm shelter or the basement of a well-built building.**

All year round, most precipitation begins in clouds as snow. If the air is colder than 0°C all the way to the ground, the precipitation falls as snow. Snow falls in California only at high elevation. The snowmelt in the spring is useful as a source of fresh water for a variety of needs, including irrigation and electricity production. **If you are caught in a snowstorm, try to find shelter from the wind.**

A **hurricane** is a tropical cyclone that has winds of 119 kilometers per hour or higher. **A hurricane begins over warm ocean water as a low-pressure area, or tropical disturbance.** If the tropical disturbance grows in size and strength, it becomes a tropical storm, which may then become a hurricane. The center of a hurricane is a ring of clouds surrounding a quiet "eye." The low pressure and high winds of the hurricane over the ocean raise the level of the water up to six meters above normal sea level. The result is a **storm surge,** a "dome" of water that sweeps across the coast where the hurricane lands. A "hurricane warning" means that hurricane conditions are expected within 24 hours. **If you hear a hurricane warning and are told to evacuate, leave the area immediately.**

Weather · *Reading/Notetaking Guide*

Storms (pp. 318–325)

This section explains how thunderstorms, tornadoes, snowstorms, and hurricanes form. The section also describes how people can stay safe in the different types of storms.

Use Target Reading Skills

As you read about how hurricanes form, fill in the flowchart to show the sequence of events.

Hurricane Formation

It begins as a low-pressure area over warm water, or a tropical disturbance.

↓

Warm, humid air rises and begins to spiral.

↓

a.

↓

b.

Introduction (p. 318)

1. What is a storm?

_____

_____

_____

Thunderstorms (pp. 319–320)

2. Circle the letter of the type of clouds in which thunderstorms form.
   a. cumulus
   b. nimbus
   c. nimbostratus
   d. cumulonimbus

3. A sudden electric discharge between parts of a cloud, between nearby clouds, or between a cloud and the ground is called

   _____.

Weather • *Reading/Notetaking Guide*

4. Circle the letter of each sentence that is true about thunder.
   a. It causes lighting to occur.
   b. You hear it after you see the lightning that caused it.
   c. It occurs because lightning heats the air.
   d. It occurs because light travels faster than sound.

5. Complete the flowchart to show the sequence of events describing how a thunderstorm can form.

   ```
   ┌──────────────────────────────────────────────────────────┐
   │ 1. Warm air is forced upward along a(n)  a. _____ front. │
   └──────────────────────────────────────────────────────────┘
                              │
                              ▼
   ┌──────────────────────────────────────────────────────────┐
   │ 2. As the air rises, it  b. _____ │
   └──────────────────────────────────────────────────────────┘
                              │
                              ▼
   ┌──────────────────────────────────────────────────────────┐
   │ 3. c. _____ falls.      │
   └──────────────────────────────────────────────────────────┘
   ```

6. Name a benefit that river floods can provide.
   _____
   _____

7. Circle the letter of each sentence that is a way to stay safe in a thunderstorm.
   a. Avoid touching electrical appliances.
   b. Get out of the water if you are swimming.
   c. Don't use the telephone.
   d. Get out of your car and go under a tree.

Tornadoes (pp. 320–321)

8. What is a tornado?
   _____
   _____
   _____

9. Is the following sentence true or false? Tornadoes develop in the same type of clouds that bring thunderstorms.
   _____

Weather ▪ *Reading/Notetaking Guide*

Storms *(continued)*

10. Circle the letter of each sentence that is true about where and when tornadoes occur.

    a. Tornadoes are most likely in late summer and early fall.

    b. Tornadoes occur often in the Great Plains.

    c. Tornadoes occur infrequently in California.

    d. Tornadoes occur in just a few parts of the United States.

11. Where is the safest place to be during a tornado?

_____

_____

_____

Snowstorms *(pp. 322–323)*

12. Under what conditions can snow fall?

_____

_____

_____

13. Circle the letter of each way that Californians might use snow.

    a. drinking water

    b. irrigation

    c. electricity

    d. recreation

14. What should you do if you are caught in a snowstorm?

_____

_____

_____

_____

Weather ▪ *Reading/Notetaking Guide*

Hurricanes (pp. 324–325)

15. Circle the letter of each sentence that is true about a hurricane.

   a. It is a tropical storm.
   b. It has winds of at least 320 kilometers per hour.
   c. It is typically about 60 kilometers across.
   d. It forms over water.

16. The center of a hurricane is called the _____.

17. Is the following sentence true or false? Hurricanes do not last as long as other storms.

   _____

18. A "dome" of water that sweeps across the coast where the hurricane lands is called a(n) _____.

19. Is the following sentence true or false? If you hear a hurricane warning and are told to evacuate, you should leave the area immediately.

   _____

Predicting the Weather

Key Concepts

■ How do weather forecasters predict the weather?

■ What can be learned from the information on weather maps?

Meteorologists are scientists who study the causes of weather and try to predict it. **Meteorologists use maps, charts, and computers to analyze weather data and to prepare weather forecasts.**

Instruments carried by balloons, satellites, and weather stations provide the data necessary to forecast the weather. Radar can be used to track rain clouds or tornadoes. The National Weather Service provides most of the weather data used by meteorologists.

A weather map is a "snapshot" of conditions at a particular time over a large area. There are many different types of weather maps. Data from weather stations all over the country are assembled into weather maps at the National Weather Service.

Maps in newspapers are simplified versions of maps produced by the National Weather Service. On some weather maps, curved lines connect places with the same air pressure or temperature. **Isobars** are lines joining places on a map that have the same air pressure. **Isotherms** are lines joining places that have the same temperature. **Standard symbols on weather maps show fronts, areas of high and low pressure, types of precipitation, and temperatures.**

A small change in the weather today can mean a larger change in the weather a week later! This is the so-called "butterfly effect."

Weather · *Reading/Notetaking Guide*

Predicting the Weather (pp. 328–332)

This section explains how weather forecasters predict the weather and why it is difficult to predict the weather accurately. The section also explains how to read weather maps.

Use Target Reading Skills

As you read about some types of weather map symbols, complete the compare-and-contrast table below.

What Symbol Represents	Type Shown	Example
Front	Cold front	
	Warm front	a.
	Stationary front	b.
	Occluded front	c.
Pressure Area	High pressure area	d.
	Low pressure area	e.
Precipitation	Drizzle	f.
	Hail	g.
	Rain	h.
	Sleet	i.
	Snow	j.

Weather · *Reading/Notetaking Guide*

Predicting the Weather *(continued)*

Weather Forecasting (p. 329)

1. Scientists who study the causes of weather and try to predict it are called

    _____.

2. Circle the letter of each choice that is a source of weather information for meteorologists.

    a. radar

    b. seismographs

    c. instruments carried by balloons

    d. satellites

Reading Weather Maps (pp. 330–332)

3. What data are indicated by symbols on a weather map?

    _____

    _____

    _____

    _____

4. What are the temperature, air pressure, and wind direction at the weather station represented by the symbol shown here?

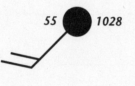

    _____

    _____

    _____

Match the term with its definition.

Term	Definition
____ **5.** isobars	**a.** Lines on a weather map joining places that have the same temperature
____ **6.** isotherms	**b.** Lines on a weather map joining places that have the same air pressure

Weather ▪ *Reading/Notetaking Guide*

7. What do standard symbols show on weather maps in newspapers?

_____

_____

_____

_____

_____

8. Is the following sentence true or false? The "butterfly effect" refers to the fact that a small change in the weather today can mean a larger change in the weather a week later.

_____

Chapter 9 Climate and Climate Change · *Section 1 Summary*

What Causes Climate?

Key Concepts

- What factors influence temperature?

- What factors influence precipitation?

- What causes the seasons?

Climate is the long-term, average conditions of temperature, precipitation, winds, and clouds in an area. The climate of a region is determined by two main factors: temperature and precipitation.

The same factors that affect climate regions also affect small areas. **Microclimates** are small areas with climate conditions that differ from those around them.

The main factors that influence temperature are latitude, altitude, distance from large bodies of water, and ocean currents. Earth's surface is divided into three temperature zones. The **tropical zone** is the area near the equator, between about 23.5° north latitude and 23.5° south latitude. It has a warm climate because it receives direct sunlight all year. The **polar zones** extend from about 66.5° to 90° north and 66.5° to 90° south latitudes. They have cold climates because the sun strikes the ground at a lower angle. The **temperate zones** are between the tropical and polar zones—from about 23.5° to 66.5° north and 23.5° to 66.5° south latitudes. They have weather that ranges from warm in the summer to cold in the winter. Altitude is an important climate factor because air temperature decreases as altitude increases. Large bodies of water influence temperatures because water heats up and cools down more slowly than land. **Marine climates** have relatively warm winters and cool summers. **Continental climates** occur in inland areas and are often characterized by cold winters and warm or hot summers. Many marine climates are also influenced by ocean currents. **Ocean currents** are streams of water within the oceans that move in regular patterns.

The main factors that affect precipitation are prevailing winds, the presence of mountains, and seasonal winds. A mountain range in the path of prevailing winds influences where precipitation falls. Winds are forced to rise and pass over the mountains. The rising warm air cools, and its water vapor condenses and falls as rain or snow on the **windward** side of the mountains, the side the oncoming wind hits. The land on the **leeward,** or downwind, side of mountains receives little precipitation. Sea and land breezes over a large region that change direction with the seasons are called **monsoons.**

Most places on Earth, outside the tropics, have four seasons. **The seasons are caused by the tilt of Earth's axis as Earth travels around the sun.** The seasons change as the amount of energy each hemisphere receives from the sun changes. For example, in June the north end of Earth's axis is tilted toward the sun. The Northern Hemisphere receives more energy. It is summer in the Northern Hemisphere and winter in the Southern Hemisphere.

What Causes Climate? (pp. 346–353)

This section describes factors that determine climate, or an area's long-term, average weather conditions. The section also explains what causes the seasons.

Use Target Reading Skills

Look at the illustration titled Rain Shadow on pages 350–351 of your textbook. In the graphic organizer below, ask three questions that you have about the illustration. As you read about the factors that affect precipitation, write answers to your questions.

Rain Shadow
Q: How do mountain ranges affect climate?
A:
Q:
A:
Q:
A:

Introduction (p. 346)

1. The long-term, average conditions of temperature, precipitation, winds, and clouds in an area is its _____.

2. A small area with climate conditions that differ from those around it is called a(n) _____.

Factors Affecting Temperature (pp. 347–349)

3. What are the main factors that influence temperature?

   _____

   _____

   _____

4. It is colder at high latitudes because the sun's rays strike Earth's surface at a(n) _____ angle there.

Climate and Climate Change · *Reading/Notetaking Guide*

What Causes Climate? *(continued)*

5. List the three temperature zones on Earth's surface that are based on latitude.

    a. _____   b. _____

    c. _____

6. Complete the following compare-and-contrast table to show the relationship among temperature zones, latitude, and angle of the sun's rays.

Temperature Zone	Latitude Is Between	Angle of Sun's Rays
a. _____	23.5° north and b. _____	Direct or nearly direct all year round
Temperate	c. _____ and 23.5° to 66.5° south	More direct in the summer; Less direct in d. _____
e. _____	f. _____ _____	Less direct all year round

g. Use the chart to write one or two sentences about the relationship between latitude and the angle of the sun's rays.

_____

_____

_____

_____

h. Is the climate of a temperate zone in summer more like a polar zone or a tropical zone? Use the information in the table to explain your answer.

_____

_____

_____

_____

7. Is the following sentence true or false? Areas at high altitudes have cool climates, no matter what their latitude.

_____

Climate and Climate Change ▪ *Reading/Notetaking Guide*

Match the type of climate with its description.

Type of Climate	Description
____ **8.** marine climate	**a.** Relatively warm winters and cool summers
____ **9.** continental climate	**b.** Cold winters and warm or hot summers

10. Circle the letter of each sentence that is true about how ocean currents influence climates.

    a. Ocean currents influence many marine climates.

    b. Only warm ocean currents influence climates.

    c. The North Atlantic Drift gives Ireland a warm climate for its latitude.

    d. The California Current gives the West Coast a warm climate for its latitude.

Factors Affecting Precipitation (pp. 350–351)

11. List the main factors that affect precipitation.

    a. _____   **b.** _____

    c. _____

12. Is the following sentence true or false? Winds blowing inland from oceans carry less water than winds blowing from land.

    _____

13. Circle the letter of each sentence that is true about the effect of mountain ranges on precipitation.

    a. Precipitation falls mainly on the leeward side of mountains.

    b. The windward side of mountains is in a rain shadow.

    c. As air rises to pass over a mountain range, its water vapor condenses, forming clouds.

    d. Precipitation usually falls on the side of the mountains that is hit by oncoming wind.

14. Sea and land breezes over a large region that change direction with the seasons are called _____.

Climate and Climate Change · *Reading/Notetaking Guide*

What Causes Climate? *(continued)*

The Seasons *(pp. 352–353)*

15. Is the following sentence true or false? It is colder in the winter in the Northern Hemisphere because Earth is farther from the sun then.

_____

16. When Earth is in the position shown in the drawing, what season is it in the Northern Hemisphere?

_____

_____

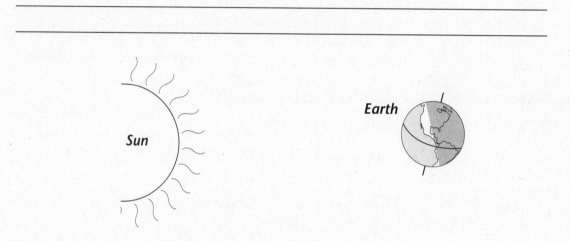

17. Circle the letter of each sentence that is true about Earth's axis.

   a. The axis always points in the same direction.
   b. The north end of the axis is tilted away from the sun all year.
   c. When it is summer in the Southern Hemisphere, the south end of the axis is tilted toward the sun.
   d. In March and September, neither end of the axis is tilted toward the sun.

18. Why is Earth's surface warmer in the Northern Hemisphere when it is summer there?

_____

_____

_____

Currents and Climate

Key Concepts

- What causes surface currents and deep currents, and what effects do they have?
- What are El Niño and La Niña?
- How does upwelling affect the distribution of nutrients in the ocean?

Currents are large streams of moving water that flow through the oceans. Unlike waves, currents carry water great distances. Some currents move water at the surface of the ocean. Other currents move water deep below the surface.

Surface currents, which affect water to a depth of several hundred meters, are driven mainly by winds. Therefore, surface currents follow the major wind patterns of the globe, moving in a circular pattern in the major oceans. The Coriolis effect, which is the effect of Earth's rotation on the direction of winds and currents, is the reason for this circular pattern. The Coriolis effect causes currents to curve to the right in the Northern Hemisphere and to the left in the Southern Hemisphere.

Climate is the pattern of temperature and precipitation typical of an area over a long period of time. Currents affect climate by moving cold and warm water around the globe. **A surface current warms or cools the air above it, influencing the climate of the land near the coast.** The California Current in summer and the Davidson Current in winter help to moderate coastal climates in California.

El Niño and La Niña are short-term changes in the tropical Pacific Ocean caused by changes in ocean surface currents and prevailing winds. El Niño is a warm-water event that causes the surface of the ocean in the eastern Pacific to be unusually warm. It affects weather patterns around the world and is associated with heavy rains, flooding, and mudslides in California. **La Niña** occurs when the waters in the eastern Pacific are colder than normal.

Deep currents are caused by differences in the density of ocean water. Density, in turn, depends on temperature and salinity. **Salinity** is the total amount of dissolved salts in a water sample. When ice forms near the poles, the salinity of the remaining liquid water increases. This cold, salty water is dense and sinks, flowing along the ocean floor as a deep current. **Deep currents move and mix water around the world. They carry cold water from the poles toward the equator.** They flow much more slowly than surface currents.

Another type of water movement is **upwelling.** This is the upward movement of cold water from the ocean depths to replace warm surface water moved away by winds. **Upwelling brings up tiny ocean organisms, minerals, and other nutrients from the deeper layers of the water.** Without this motion, the surface waters of the open ocean would be very scarce in nutrients. Areas of upwelling usually attract huge schools of fish that feed on these nutrients.

Climate and Climate Change ▪ *Reading/Notetaking Guide*

Currents and Climate (pp. 356–361)

This section describes surface and deep ocean currents and explains how they affect climate.

Use Target Reading Skills

Read the section "Surface Currents," and complete the outline below.

Surface Currents

I. Introduction

   A. Surface currents are driven mainly by wind.

II.

   A. Causes surface currents to curve to the right in the Northern Hemisphere and to the left in the Southern Hemisphere

     1.

III.

   A. The cool, south-flowing California Current cools the climate in California's coastal areas.

   B.

   C.

Introduction (p. 356)

1. A large stream of moving water that flows through the oceans is a(n) _____.

2. Is the following sentence true or false? Currents can carry water great distances.

    _____

Surface Currents (pp. 357–358)

3. Circle the letter of each sentence that is true about surface currents.

    a. They affect water down to 2 kilometers.

    b. They are driven mainly by winds.

    c. They move in circular patterns.

    d. They occur only in the Pacific Ocean.

Climate and Climate Change · *Reading/Notetaking Guide*

4. The effect of Earth's rotation on the direction of winds and currents is called the _____.

5. Is the following sentence true or false? In the Northern Hemisphere, surface currents curve to the left.

   _____

6. Due to the Coriolis effect, the Gulf Stream curves _____ across the Atlantic Ocean.

7. Circle the letter of each sentence that is true about the California Current.

   a. It flows all year long.
   b. It flows southward from southern Canada.
   c. It is a cool-water current.
   d. It makes summer climates cooler along the West Coast.

8. Is the following sentence true or false? A surface current warms or cools the air above it, influencing the climate of the land near the coast.

   _____

El Niño and La Niña (p. 359)

9. What causes El Niño or La Niña to form?

   _____

   _____

10. Is the following sentence true or false? El Niño and La Niña influence weather only along the West Coast of the United States.

    _____

11. Circle the letter of each sentence that is true about El Niño.

    a. It begins when an unusual pattern of winds forms over the western Pacific.
    b. It occurs approximately every twelve years.
    c. It causes the surface of the ocean in the eastern Pacific to be unusually warm.
    d. It is associated with heavy rains, flooding, and mudslides in California.

12. Is the following sentence true or false? A La Niña event is the opposite of an El Niño event.

    _____

13. Circle the letter of each sentence that is true about La Niña.

    a. It begins when surface waters in the eastern Pacific are colder than normal.
    b. It is a warm-water event.
    c. It brings colder winters and greater precipitation to the Pacific Northwest.
    d. It causes decreased hurricane activity in the western Atlantic.

Climate and Climate Change · *Reading/Notetaking Guide*

Currents and Climate *(continued)*

Deep Currents (p. 360)

14. What are deep currents and how do they form?

_____

_____

_____

_____

15. The total amount of dissolved salts in a water sample is its

_____.

16. Circle the letter of each sentence that is true about the formation of deep currents.

    a. Warm surface currents from the equator cool as they approach the poles.

    b. As ice forms near the poles, the salinity of the water decreases.

    c. The cooler, saltier water sinks.

    d. The cold water flows back to the equator along the ocean floor.

17. Deep currents move and mix water around the world. They carry _____ water from the poles toward the

_____.

18. Circle the letter of each sentence that is true about deep currents.

    a. They can be thought of as a global conveyer belt.

    b. It takes them about ten years to flow from the pole to the equator and back.

    c. They transfer heat through the ocean.

    d. They bring dissolved oxygen down into the ocean depths.

Climate and Climate Change ▪ *Reading/Notetaking Guide*

Upwelling (p. 361)

19. The upward movement of cold water from the ocean depths is referred to as _____.

20. Is the following sentence true or false? Upwelling is caused by tides.

_____

21. Label the wind, warm surface water, and the area of upwelling in the diagram below.

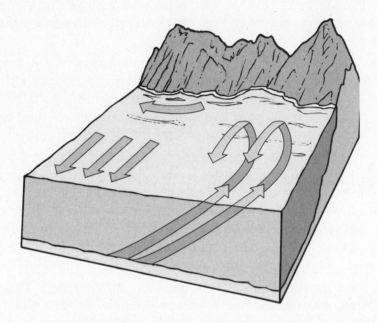

22. Why are upwelling zones usually home to enormous schools of fish?

_____

_____

_____

Chapter 9 Climate and Climate Change · *Section 3 Summary*

Climate Regions

Key Concepts

- What factors are used to classify climates?

- What are the six main climate regions?

Scientists classify climates using a system developed by Wladimir Köppen around 1900. **Scientists classify climates according to two major factors: temperature and precipitation.** The Köppen system identifies broad climate regions. **There are six main climate regions: tropical rainy, dry, temperate marine, temperate continental, polar, and highlands.**

The tropics have two types of rainy climates: tropical wet and tropical wet-and-dry. Tropical wet climates have year-round heat and heavy rainfall. Dense forests grow in tropical wet climates. **Rain forests** have large amounts of rain fall year-round. Tropical wet-and-dry climates have less rainfall and distinct dry and rainy seasons. Tropical grasslands, called **savannas,** are found in tropical wet-and-dry climates.

Dry climates are located in areas where the amount of precipitation is less than the amount of water that could potentially evaporate. Dry climates often lie far from oceans or in the rain shadows of mountains. **Dry climates include arid and semiarid climates.** Arid regions, or **deserts,** get less than 25 centimeters of rain every year. Deserts also have extreme hot and cold temperatures. Semiarid regions, or **steppes,** are usually located on the edges of deserts. A steppe gets enough rainfall for short grasses and low bushes to grow.

Temperate marine climates are humid and have mild winters. **There are three kinds of temperate marine climates: marine west coast, Mediterranean, and humid subtropical.** Marine west coast climates are the coolest temperate marine climates. Humid ocean air brings cool, rainy summers and mild, rainy winters. Mediterranean climates are drier and warmer. In winter, ocean air masses bring cool, rainy weather. Summers are warmer and drier. **Chaparral,** areas with dense shrubs and small trees, are found here. **Humid subtropical** climates are wet and warm, but not as constantly hot as the tropics.

Temperate continental climates are only found on continents in the Northern Hemisphere, and include humid continental and subarctic. Humid continental climates have constantly changing weather. In winter, the weather is bitterly cold with some rain or snow. Summers are hot with high humidity and moderate rainfall. The **subarctic** climates lie north of the humid continental climates. Summers are short and cool. Winters are long and bitterly cold.

The polar climate is the coldest climate region, and includes the ice cap and tundra climates. Ice cap and tundra climates are found only near the poles. Ice caps are covered with ice and snow, and temperatures are always at or below freezing. The **tundra** climate region stretches across northern Alaska, Canada, and Russia. It has short, cool summers followed by bitterly cold winters. Some layers of the tundra soil, called **permafrost,** are always frozen.

Temperature falls as altitude increases, so highland regions are colder than the regions that surround them. Increasing altitude produces climate changes similar to the climate change you would expect with increasing latitude.

Climate and Climate Change · *Reading/Notetaking Guide*

Climate Regions (pp. 362–371)

This section explains how scientists classify climates and describes six major climate regions.

Use Target Reading Skills

Read the introductory section at the start of the section "Climate Regions." Then, complete the outline below.

Climate Regions

I. Factors Affecting How Climates Are Categorized

    A. Temperature

    B.

II. Climate Regions

    A.

    B.

    C.

    D.

    E.

    F.

Introduction (p. 362)

1. What are the two major factors that scientists use to classify climates?

   _____

2. List the six major climate regions.

   a. _____ b. _____

   c. _____ d. _____

   e. _____ f. _____

3. Is the following sentence true or false? Climate regions are marked by clear boundaries.

   _____

Climate and Climate Change · *Reading/Notetaking Guide*

Climate Regions *(continued)*

Tropical Rainy Climates *(pp. 363–365)*

4. Circle the letter of each sentence that is true about a tropical wet climate.

    a. It has heavy rainfall year-round.

    b. It is hot year-round.

    c. Rain forests grow in this type of climate.

    d. Florida has this type of climate.

5. Circle the letter of each sentence that is true about a tropical wet-and-dry climate.

    a. It has a rainy season and a dry season.

    b. It is hot year-round.

    c. Grasslands grow in this type of climate.

    d. Hawaii has this type of climate.

Dry Climates *(p. 366)*

6. Arid regions, which get less than 25 centimeters of rain every year, are also called _____.

7. Where are arid climates in California?

    _____

    _____

    _____

8. An area that is dry but gets enough rainfall for short grasses and low bushes to grow is called a(n) _____.

9. The steppe region of the United States is the _____.

Temperate Marine Climates *(pp. 367–368)*

10. Complete the compare/contrast table showing the different types of marine climates.

Temperate Marine Climates		
Type of Climate	**Characteristics**	**U.S. Region**
a. _____	Cool and wet	Pacific Northwest
Mediterranean	**b.** _____	**c.** _____
d. _____	Warm and wet	**e.** _____

    f. Write a sentence that describes the relationship between location and temperature of two regions in the United States with a temperate marine climate.

_____

_____

_____

Temperate Continental Climates (p. 369)

11. Circle the letter of each sentence that is true about temperate continental climates.

    a. They are found in both the Northern and Southern Hemispheres.
    b. They are greatly influenced by oceans.
    c. They have extremes of temperature.
    d. They are found in the northeastern United States.

12. Is the following sentence true or false? Humid continental climates receive less precipitation in summer than in winter.

_____

13. What are summers and winters like in subarctic climates?

_____

_____

_____

Polar Climates (p. 370)

14. Is the following sentence true or false? The polar climate is the coldest climate region.

_____

15. Is the following sentence true or false? Plants cannot grow in ice cap climates.

_____

16. Permanently frozen tundra soil is called _____.

Highlands (p. 371)

17. How do highland climates differ from climates of the regions that surround them?

_____

_____

_____

18. The climate above the tree line is like that of the _____.

Climate Change

Key Concepts

- How might human activities be affecting the temperature of Earth's atmosphere?

- How have human activities affected the ozone layer?

Throughout Earth's history, climates have gradually changed. Over millions of years, warm periods have alternated with cold periods known as **ice ages,** or glacial episodes. During each ice age, glaciers covered large parts of Earth's surface.

Most past changes in world climates were caused by natural factors. But recently scientists have observed climate changes that could be the result of human activities. For example, over the last 120 years, the average temperature of the troposphere has risen by 0.7°C. This gradual increase in the temperature of Earth's atmosphere is called **global warming.**

Gases in Earth's atmosphere hold in heat from the sun, keeping the atmosphere at a comfortable temperature for living things. The process by which gases in Earth's atmosphere trap energy is called the greenhouse effect. Gases in the atmosphere that trap energy are called **greenhouse gases.** Carbon dioxide, water vapor, and methane are some of the greenhouse gases. **Many scientists have hypothesized that human activities that add greenhouse gases to the atmosphere are warming Earth's atmosphere.**

Many scientists think that an increase in carbon dioxide is a major factor in global warming. Since the late 1800s, the level of carbon dioxide in the atmosphere has increased steadily. This increase could be due to human activities such as the burning of wood, coal, oil, and natural gas. Other scientists think that the warming of Earth is a natural variation in the climate.

The effects of global warming are not known. The possible effects might include increased farming in some areas, destruction of fertile land in other areas, increased hurricane strength, and flooding of low-lying coastal areas due to increased sea levels caused by melting glaciers and polar ice caps.

Another global change in the atmosphere involves the ozone layer. **Chemicals produced by humans have been damaging the ozone layer.** A large area of reduced ozone, or **ozone hole,** was being created. A major cause of the ozone depletion is a group of compounds called **chlorofluorocarbons,** or CFCs. CFCs can last decades and rise all the way to the stratosphere. In the stratosphere, ultraviolet radiation breaks down the CFC molecules into atoms, including chlorine. The chlorine atoms then break ozone down into oxygen atoms. A decrease in ozone results in an increase in the amount of ultraviolet radiation that reaches Earth. Ultraviolet radiation can cause eye damage and several kinds of skin cancer. In the United States, it will take until 2010 to completely eliminate the use of CFCs.

Climate and Climate Change · *Reading/Notetaking Guide*

Climate Change (pp. 374–379)

This section explains how human activities may be increasing Earth's temperature by changing the atmosphere.

Use Target Reading Skills

Complete the first column in the chart by filling in the red headings. Then in the second column, ask a what, how, *or* where *question for each heading. As you read the section, complete the third column with the answers.*

Section 4: Climate Change		
Heading	**Question**	**Answer**

Introduction (p. 374)

1. Over millions of years, warm periods have alternated with cold periods known as _____.

2. Each ice age lasted _____ years or longer.

Global Warming (pp. 375–377)

3. Is the following sentence true or false? Over the last 120 years, the average temperature of the troposphere has risen by about 0.7°C.

   _____

Match the term with its definition.

Term

____ 4. greenhouse effect

____ 5. global warming

Definition

a. Process by which Earth's atmosphere traps solar energy

b. Gradual increase in the temperature of Earth's atmosphere

6. Gases in the atmosphere that trap solar energy are called _____.

Climate and Climate Change · *Reading/Notetaking Guide*

Climate Change (continued)

7. Name three greenhouse gases.

_____

_____

_____

8. How may human activities be warming Earth's atmosphere?

_____

_____

_____

_____

9. Circle the letter of each choice that is the outcome of burning wood, coal, oil, and natural gas.

   a. Carbon dioxide is added to the air.
   b. Global warming is prevented.
   c. Less heat is trapped by Earth's atmosphere.
   d. The amount of carbon dioxide in the air decreases.

10. Is the following sentence true or false? The amount of carbon dioxide in the air has been steadily increasing. _____

11. Is the following sentence true or false? Everyone agrees about the causes of global warming. _____

12. How might changes in solar energy affect Earth's climate?

_____

_____

_____

13. Circle the letter of each choice that is thought to be a possible effect of global warming.

   a. Places too cold for farming today could become farmland.
   b. Fertile fields might become "dust bowls."
   c. Sea levels would drop.
   d. Low-lying coastal areas might be flooded.

Ozone Depletion (pp. 378–379)

14. Is the following sentence true or false? Ozone in the stratosphere filters out much of the harmful ultraviolet radiation from the sun.

_____

15. Is the following sentence true or false? The ozone hole over Antarctica continues to grow each year. _____

Climate and Climate Change ▪ *Reading/Notetaking Guide*

16. What are chlorofluorocarbons, or CFCs?

_____

_____

_____

17. Complete the flowchart.

CFCs and Ozone Depletion

CFCs are released into air.

↓

CFCs rise to the **a.** _____ .

↓

CFCs break down into chlorine atoms.

↓

b. _____ atoms break down ozone into **c.** _____ atoms.

↓

Less ozone is available to block
d. _____ .

e. Where in the atmosphere is ozone broken down by CFCs?

_____

f. Suppose CFCs were completely eliminated. Using the flowchart, explain how
the amount of ultraviolet light reaching Earth would change and why.

_____

_____

_____

18. What have the United States and other countries done to prevent ozone
depletion?

_____

_____

_____

Chapter 10 Ecosystems ▪ *Section 1 Summary*

Living Things and the Environment

Key Concepts

- What needs are met by an organism's environment?

- What are the two parts of an organism's habitat with which it interacts?

- What are the levels of organization within an ecosystem?

A prairie dog is one type of **organism,** or living thing. Different types of organisms live in different types of environments. **An organism obtains food, water, shelter, and other things it needs to live, grow, and reproduce from its environment.** Other living things depend on plants and algae for food. An environment that provides the things the organism needs to live, grow, and reproduce is called its **habitat.**

An organism interacts with both living and nonliving parts of its habitat. The living parts of a habitat are called **biotic factors.** The nonliving parts of a habitat are called **abiotic factors.** Abiotic factors include water, sunlight, oxygen, temperature, and soil. Some organisms make their own food in a process called **photosynthesis.**

A **species** is a group of organisms that are physically similar and can mate with each other and produce offspring that can also mate and reproduce. All the members of one species in a particular area are referred to as a **population.** All the different populations that live together in an area make up a **community.** The community of organisms that live in a particular area, along with their nonliving surroundings, make up an **ecosystem. The smallest level of organization is a single organism, which belongs to a population that includes other members of its species. The population belongs to a community of different species. The community and abiotic factors together form an ecosystem.**

The study of how living things interact with each other and with their environment is called **ecology.** Ecologists are scientists who study ecology. They study how organisms react to changes in their environment.

Ecosystems · *Reading/Notetaking Guide*

Living Things and the Environment (pp. 392–396)

This section describes what organisms need and how their environments provide for their needs. The section also describes how organisms live together in populations and communities.

Use Target Reading Skills

As you read the "Habitats" section, write the main idea—the biggest or most important idea—in the graphic organizer below. Then write three supporting details that give examples of the main idea.

Main Idea

An organism obtains food, . . .

Detail	**Detail**	**Detail**

Habitats (p. 393)

1. A(n) _____ obtains food, water, shelter, and other things it needs to live, grow, and reproduce from its environment.

2. The place where an organism lives and that provides the things the organism needs is called its _____.

3. What needs of an organism are provided by its habitat?

   _____

4. Is the following sentence true or false? An area contains only one habitat.

   _____

Ecosystems ▪ *Reading/Notetaking Guide*

Living Things and the Environment *(continued)*

Biotic Factors *(p. 393)*

5. The living parts of a habitat are called _____.

6. Circle the letter of each choice that is a biotic factor in a prairie dog ecosystem.

   a. Grass and other plants that the prairie dog eats
   b. Hawks, ferrets, and other animals that hunt the prairie dog
   c. The soil that provides the prairie dog with a home
   d. Worms, fungi, and bacteria that also live in the soil

Abiotic Factors *(p. 394)*

7. The nonliving parts of a habitat are called _____.

8. Complete the concept map.

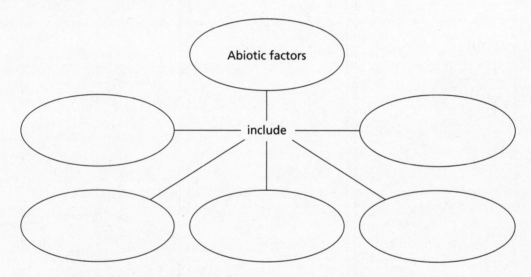

9. Circle the letter of each sentence that is true about water.

   a. It is needed by all living things.
   b. It makes up 95 percent of the human body.
   c. It is needed by algae and plants to make food.
   d. It is an abiotic factor only for organisms that actually live in the water.

10. The process in which plants and algae make food using water, sunlight, and carbon dioxide is called _____.

Ecosystems · *Reading/Notetaking Guide*

11. Circle the letter of each sentence that is true about oxygen.

    a. Humans can live only a few hours without it.
    b. Organisms that live on land get it from the air.
    c. It makes up about 40 percent of air.
    d. Fish get it from the water around them.

Levels of Organization (pp. 395–397)

12. What is a species?

    _____

    _____

    _____

    _____

    _____

    _____

13. Circle the letter of each choice that is an example of a population.

    a. all the prairie dogs in a prairie dog town
    b. all the bees in a hive
    c. all the pigeons in New York City
    d. all the trees in a forest

14. Is the following sentence true or false? All populations live in the same-sized area.

    _____

15. All the different populations that live together in an area make up a(n)

    _____.

16. Circle the letter of the choice that lists the levels of organization in an ecosystem from the smallest unit of organization to the largest.

    a. population, organism, community, ecosystem
    b. organism, population, ecosystem, community
    c. organism, community, population, ecosystem
    d. organism, population, community, ecosystem

Ecosystems · *Reading/Notetaking Guide*

Living Things and the Environment *(continued)*

17. Is the following sentence true or false? To be considered a community, populations must live close enough together to interact.

_____

18. In addition to a community of different species, what else does an ecosystem include?

_____

_____

_____

_____

_____

Populations

Key Concepts

■ What causes populations to change in size?

■ What factors limit population growth?

Ecologists study populations to determine how a population may be changing. This is done by observing population changes over several years.

Populations can change in size when new members join the population or when members leave the population. The main way in which new individuals are added to a population is being born in it. The **birth rate** of a population is the number of births in a population over a certain amount of time. The major way that individuals leave a population is by dying. The **death rate** is the number of deaths in a population over a certain amount of time. If the birth rate is greater than the death rate, the population will generally increase in size. If the death rate is greater than the birth rate, the population size will generally decrease. The size of a population can also change when individuals move into or out of the population. **Immigration** means moving into a population. **Emigration** means leaving a population. Graphs are useful to show changes in the size of a population over time.

A **limiting factor** is an environmental factor that causes a population to stop growing. **Some limiting factors for populations are food and water, space, light, soil composition, and weather conditions.** The largest population that an environment can support is called the **carrying capacity.** A population usually stays near its carrying capacity because of the limiting factors in its habitat.

Ecosystems · *Reading/Notetaking Guide*

Populations (pp. 399–403)

This section describes how scientists study population density, size, and growth. The section also explains how factors such as food, space, and weather limit how large populations can become.

Use Target Reading Skills

Complete the first column in the chart by filling in the red headings. Then in the second column, ask a what, how, *or* where *question for each heading. As you read the section, complete the third column with the answers.*

Section 2: Populations

Heading	Question	Answer

Introduction (p. 399)

1. How do ecologists determine if a population is changing?

_____

_____

_____

_____

_____

_____

_____

Ecosystems · *Reading/Notetaking Guide*

Changes in Population Size (pp. 400–401)

2. How can populations change in size?

_____

_____

_____

_____

3. What is the main way in which new individuals join a population?

_____

_____

_____

4. The number of births in a population over a certain amount of time is the
_____.

5. What is the main way that individuals leave a population?

_____

_____

_____

_____

6. The number of deaths in a population over a certain amount of time is
the _____.

7. Is the following sentence true or false? If the birth rate is greater than the
death rate, population size decreases.

_____

Match the term with its definition.

Term

____ 8. immigration

____ 9. emigration

Definition

a. Leaving a population

b. Moving into a population

10. Is the following sentence true or false? Population density is the number
of individuals in a specific area.

_____

11. How can a graph be used to show population changes?

_____

_____

_____

Ecosystems • *Reading/Notetaking Guide*

Populations *(continued)*

Limiting Factors *(pp. 402–403)*

12. An environmental factor that causes a population to decrease is called a(n) _____.

13. What are some limiting factors for populations?

   _____

   _____

   _____

14. The largest population that an area can support is called its

   _____.

15. Is the following sentence true or false? Space is often a limiting factor for plants.

   _____

16. Which of the following is NOT a limiting factor in soil composition?
   a. mineral content
   b. acidity
   c. humus
   d. litter

17. What are some ways weather conditions can limit population growth?

   _____

   _____

   _____

Energy Flow in Ecosystems

Key Concepts

- What energy roles do organisms play in an ecosystem?

- How does energy move through an ecosystem?

- How much energy is available at each level of an energy pyramid?

An organism's energy role is determined by how it obtains energy and how it interacts with the other living things in its ecosystem. **Each of the organisms in an ecosystem fills the energy role of producer, consumer, or decomposer.**

Plants, algae, and some bacteria can carry out photosynthesis. In this process, the organism uses the sun's energy to turn water and carbon dioxide into sugar molecules. An organism that can make its own food is a **producer.** Producers are the source of all the food in an ecosystem.

Other organisms cannot make their own food. They depend on producers for food and energy. An organism that obtains energy by feeding on other organisms is a **consumer.** Consumers are classified by what they eat. Consumers that eat only plants are called **herbivores.** Consumers that eat only animals are called **carnivores.** A consumer that eats both plants and animals is called an **omnivore.** A **scavenger** is a carnivore that feeds on the bodies of dead organisms. An organism may play more than one role in an ecosystem.

Organisms that break down wastes and dead organisms and return the raw materials to the environment are called **decomposers.** As decomposers obtain energy for their own needs, they return simple molecules to the environment to be used again by other organisms.

The transfer of energy from organism to organism in an ecosystem can be shown in diagrams called food chains and food webs. A **food chain** is a series of events in which one organism eats another and obtains energy. The first organism in a food chain is always a producer. The second organism, called a first-level consumer, eats the producer. The next consumer, called a second-level consumer, eats the first-level consumer. A food chain shows just one possible path of energy through an ecosystem.

Most producers and consumers are part of many food chains. A more realistic way to show the flow of energy through an ecosystem is a food web. A **food web** consists of the many overlapping food chains in an ecosystem.

When an organism makes its own food or eats other organisms, it obtains energy. The organism uses some of this energy to move, feed, grow, and reproduce. Only some of the energy will be available to the next organism in the food web. A diagram called an **energy pyramid** shows the amount of energy that moves from one feeding level to another in a food web. **The most energy is available at the producer level of the pyramid. As you move up the pyramid, each level has less energy available than the level below.** In general, only about 10 percent of the chemical energy at one level of a food web is transferred to the next higher level. As a result, there are usually few organisms at the highest level in a food web.

Ecosystems • *Reading/Notetaking Guide*

Energy Flow in Ecosystems (pp. 404–409)

This section explains the different roles that organisms play in the movement of energy through an ecosystem. The section also describes how organisms in the different roles interact to form food chains and food webs.

Use Target Reading Skills

Look at the illustration titled A Food Web on page 407 of your textbook. In the graphic organizer below, ask three questions that you have about the illustration. As you read about food chains and food webs, write the answers to your questions.

A Food Web
Q. How is a food chain related to a food web?
A.
Q. What do the levels of a food web represent?
A.
Q. What is the role of decomposers in a food web?
A.

Energy Roles (pp. 404–405)

Match the energy role with its definition.

Energy Role

_____ **1.** producer

_____ **2.** consumer

_____ **3.** decomposer

Definition

a. Organism that breaks down wastes and dead organisms

b. Organism that obtains energy by feeding on other organisms

c. Organism that can make its own food

Ecosystems ▪ *Reading/Notetaking Guide*

4. What types of organisms are producers?

   _____

   _____

5. Is the following sentence true or false? Energy enters all ecosystems as sunlight. _____

6. Is the following sentence true or false? Producers are the source of all the food in an ecosystem. _____

7. List two major groups of decomposers.

   a. _____ b. _____

8. Complete the compare/contrast table.

Types of Consumers	
Type of Consumer	**Type of Food**
a.	Only plants
Carnivore	b.
c.	Both plants and animals
d.	Dead organisms

9. Is the following sentence true or false? Decomposers return raw materials to the environment.

   _____

Food Chains and Food Webs (pp. 406–407)

10. A series of events in which one organism eats another and obtains energy is called a(n) _____.

Ecosystems · *Reading/Notetaking Guide*

Energy Flow Ecosystems *(continued)*

11. Label the producer and the first-level and second-level consumers in the food chain illustrated below.

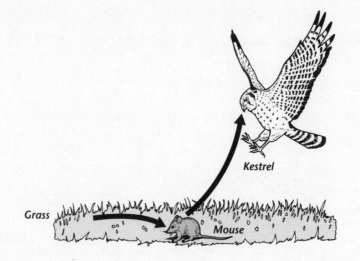

Kestrel

Grass

Mouse

12. The many overlapping food chains in an ecosystem make up a(n) _____.

13. Circle the letter of each sentence that is true about a food web.

    a. Producers are at the top of the food web.
    b. All first-level consumers are carnivores.
    c. Second-level consumers may be carnivores or omnivores.
    d. An organism may play more than one role in a food web.

Energy Pyramids (pp. 408–409)

14. What does an energy pyramid show?

_____

_____

_____

15. Circle the letter of each sentence that is true about an energy pyramid.

    a. The greatest amount of energy is available at the producer level.
    b. At each higher level of the pyramid, there is more energy available.
    c. About half the energy at one level is transferred to the next.
    d. Scavengers and decomposers are part of the energy pyramid.

16. Why are there usually few organisms at the top of a food web?

_____

_____

_____

_____

Chapter 10 Ecosystems • *Section 4 Summary*

Interactions Among Living Things

Key Concepts

- How do an organism's adaptations help it to survive?
- What are the major ways in which organisms in an ecosystem interact?
- What are the three types of symbiotic relationships?

Every organism has some unique characteristics that enable it to live in its environment. In response to their environment, species evolve, or change over time. The changes that make organisms better suited to their environment become common in that species by a process called **natural selection.** Individuals whose unique characteristics are best suited for their environment tend to survive and produce offspring. The offspring inherit those characteristics and also live to reproduce. Individuals that are poorly suited to the environment are less likely to survive and reproduce. The poorly suited characteristics may disappear from the population over time. The results of natural selection are **adaptations,** the behaviors and physical characteristics of species that allow them to live successfully in their environment.

Every organism has a variety of adaptations that are suited to its specific living conditions. These adaptations create a unique role for the organism in its ecosystem. An organism's particular role in its habitat, or how it makes its living, is called its **niche.** A niche includes the type of food the organism eats, how it obtains this food, which other organisms use the organism as food, when and how the organism reproduces, and the physical conditions it requires to survive.

Some adaptations involve how organisms interact. **There are three major types of interactions among organisms: competition, predation, and symbiosis. Competition** is the struggle between organisms to survive as they attempt to use the same limited resource. **Predation** is an interaction in which one organism kills and eats another organism. The organism that does the killing is the **predator.** The organism that is killed is the **prey.** Predators have adaptations that help them catch and kill their prey. Prey organisms have adaptations that help them avoid being caught and eaten. Predation can have a major effect on the size of a population.

Symbiosis is a close relationship between two species that benefits at least one of the species. **The three types of symbiotic relationships are mutualism, commensalism, and parasitism. Mutualism** is a relationship in which both species benefit. **Commensalism** is a relationship in which one species benefits and the other species is neither helped nor harmed. **Parasitism** involves one organism living on or inside another organism and harming it. The organism that benefits is called a **parasite,** and the organism it lives on or in is called a **host.**

Ecosystems · *Reading/Notetaking Guide*

Interactions Among Living Things (pp. 410–416)

This section explains how organisms become adapted to their environments. The section also describes three major types of interactions among organisms.

Use Target Reading Skills

Copy the compare/contrast table below into your notebook. As you read about competition, predation, and symbiosis on pages 412–416 of your textbook, complete your compare/contrast table.

Interactions Among Living Things

Type of Interaction	Description of Interaction	Effect of Interaction
Competition	In competition, organisms struggle to survive as they attempt to use the environment's limited resources, such as food, water, or shelter.	Competition limits the populations of the organisms involved because the resources for which they compete are limiting factors.
Predation		
Symbiosis • Mutualism • Commensalism • Parasitisim		

Ecosystems · *Reading/Notetaking Guide*

Adapting to the Environment (p. 411)

Match the term with its definition.

Term	Definition
Term	**Definition**
____ **1.** natural selection	**a.** Characteristic that allows a species to live successfully in its environment
____ **2.** adaptation	**b.** The way a species makes its living
____ **3.** niche	**c.** Process in which a species becomes better suited to its environment

4. Is the following sentence true or false? Every organism has a variety of adaptations that enable it to live in any kind of environment.

_____

Competition (p. 412)

5. The three major types of interactions among organisms are competition, _____, and symbiosis.

6. Is the following sentence true or false? The struggle between organisms to survive in a habitat with limited resources is called natural selection.

_____

7. Is the following sentence true or false? In a particular environment, two species can usually occupy the same niche.

_____

8. Is the following sentence true or false? Specializing can reduce competition.

_____

Ecosystems • *Reading/Notetaking Guide*

Interactions Among Living Things *(continued)*

Predation (pp. 413–414)

9. An interaction in which one organism kills and eats another is called
_____. The organism that does the killing is
the _____. The organism that is killed is the
_____.

10. Is the following sentence true or false? If a prey population decreases,
the population of its predator probably will decrease as well.
_____

11. Predators have _____ that help them catch
and kill their prey.

12. Camouflage, warning coloration, and false coloring are some adaptations
that may help organisms avoid becoming _____.

Ecosystems • *Reading/Notetaking Guide*

Symbiosis (pp. 415–416)

13. Symbiosis is a close relationship between two _____ that benefits at least one of the _____.

14. Complete the compare/contrast table.

Types of Symbiotic Relationships	
Type of Relationship	**How Species Are Affected**
Mutualism	a.
b.	One species benefits; the other species is unharmed.
c.	One species benefits; the other species is harmed.

15. In some cases of _____, two species have such a close symbiotic relationship that neither one could live without the other.

16. In a parasitic relationship, the organism that benefits is called a(n) _____, and the organism it lives on or in is called a(n) _____.

Chapter 10 Ecosystems • *Section 5 Summary*

Cycles of Matter

Key Concepts

■ What processes are involved in the water cycle?

■ How are carbon and oxygen recycled in ecosystems?

■ What is the nitrogen cycle?

Matter is recycled in ecosystems. Matter includes water, oxygen, carbon, nitrogen, and many other substances. The most important cycles of matter are the water cycle, the carbon and oxygen cycles, and the nitrogen cycle.

The water cycle is the continuous process by which water moves from Earth's surface to the atmosphere and back. **The processes of evaporation, condensation, and precipitation make up the water cycle.** Living things also contribute to the water cycle. Plants take up water through their roots and release water vapor through pores in their leaves. Animals drink water. They release water in their waste and water vapor when they exhale.

Carbon is the building block for the matter that makes up the bodies of living things. **In ecosystems, the processes by which carbon and oxygen are recycled are linked. Producers, consumers, and decomposers play roles in recycling carbon and oxygen.** Producers take in carbon dioxide from the atmosphere during photosynthesis. In this process, the producers use carbon from the carbon dioxide to produce other carbon-containing molecules. These molecules include sugars and starches. Consumers obtain energy from these molecules by breaking them down into simpler molecules. The consumers release water and carbon dioxide as waste products of the process. At the same time, producers release oxygen as a result of photosynthesis. Other organisms take in oxygen from the air or water and use it in their life processes.

Like carbon, nitrogen is a necessary building block in the matter that makes up living things. **In the nitrogen cycle, nitrogen moves from the air to the soil, into living things, and back into the air.** Most organisms cannot use nitrogen gas in the air. Nitrogen gas is called "free" nitrogen because it is not combined with other kinds of atoms. Most organisms can use nitrogen only when it has been "fixed," or combined with other elements to form nitrogen-containing compounds. The process of changing nitrogen gas into a usable form of nitrogen is called **nitrogen fixation.** Most nitrogen fixation is performed by certain kinds of bacteria. Some of these bacteria live in bumps called nodules on the roots of certain plants. Once the nitrogen has been fixed, it can be used by organisms to build proteins and other complex substances. Decomposers break down these complex compounds. Decomposition returns simple nitrogen compounds to the soil. Certain types of bacteria break down the nitrogen compounds completely. These bacteria release free nitrogen back into the air, and the cycle starts again.

Ecosystems ▪ *Reading/Notetaking Guide*

Cycles of Matter (pp. 417–421)

This section describes three cycles in nature that recycle matter in ecosystems.

Use Target Reading Skills

As you read about the nitrogen cycle, fill in the diagram to show the sequence of events.

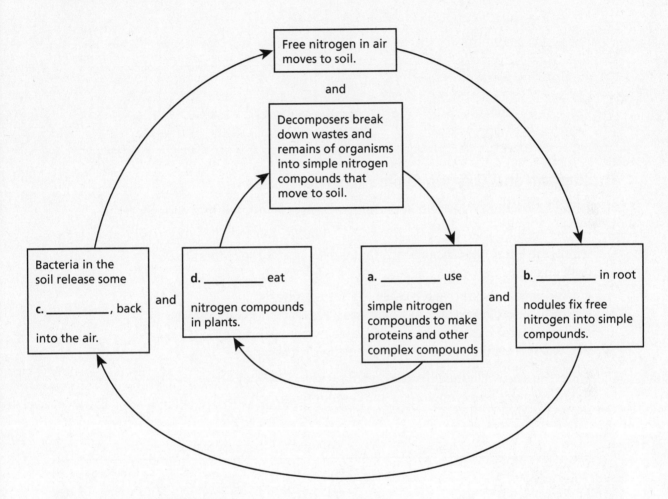

The Water Cycle (p. 417)

1. What three processes make up the water cycle?

   a._____

   b._____

   c._____

Ecosystems • *Reading/Notetaking Guide*

Cycles of Matter *(continued)*

2. Complete the table below to describe how living things affect the water cycle.

In	Out
Plants absorb water through their roots	a.
Animals drink water.	b.

The Carbon and Oxygen Cycles (pp. 418–419)

3. Is the following sentence true or false? Carbon is not necessary for life.
   _____

4. Circle the letter of each sentence that is true about the carbon and oxygen cycles.

   a. Producers take in oxygen during photosynthesis.
   b. Producers release carbon dioxide as a result of photosynthesis.
   c. Consumers release carbon dioxide as a waste product.
   d. Consumers take in oxygen for their life processes.

5. Label the arrows in the illustration below to indicate whether they show the movement of oxygen or the movement of carbon dioxide through the ecosystem.

Ecosystems · *Reading/Notetaking Guide*

The Nitrogen Cycle (pp. 420–421)

6. Is the following sentence true or false? Most organisms use nitrogen directly from the air.

    _____

7. The process of changing free nitrogen gas into a usable form of nitrogen is called _____.

8. Is the following sentence true or false? Most nitrogen fixation is performed by plants.

    _____

9. How does nitrogen return to the environment?

    _____

    _____

    _____

    _____

    _____

Changes in Communities

Key Concept

■ How do primary and secondary succession differ?

Fires, floods, volcanoes, hurricanes, and other natural disasters can change communities in a short period of time. Even without a disaster, communities change. The series of predictable changes that occur in a community over time is called **succession.**

Primary succession is the series of changes that occur in an area where no soil or organisms exist. The area might be a new island formed by the eruption of an undersea volcano or an area uncovered by a melting sheet of ice. When the land is first exposed, there is no soil. The first species to populate the area are called **pioneer species.** Pioneer species are usually lichens and mosses, which can grow on bare rocks. As they grow, the lichens and mosses help break up the rocks to form soil. When these organisms die, they provide nutrients that enrich the developing soil. Over time, seeds of plants land in the new soil and begin to grow. The specific plants that grow depend on the climate of the area. In time, as the soil grows older and richer, a mature forest may develop.

Secondary succession is the series of changes that occur in an area where the ecosystem has been disturbed, but where soil and organisms still exist. Natural disturbances include fires, hurricanes, and tornadoes. Human activities, such as farming, logging, or mining, also may disturb an ecosystem. **Unlike primary succession, secondary succession occurs in a place where an ecosystem currently exists.** Secondary succession usually occurs more rapidly than primary succession.

Changes in Communities (pp. 422–425)

This section describes a series of predictable changes that occur in a community over time.

Use Target Reading Skills

As you read about primary succession, fill in the flowchart to show the sequence of events.

Primary Succession

Volcanic Eruption: Shortly after a volcanic eruption, there is no soil, only ash and rock.

↓

Pioneer Species: **a.**

↓

b.

↓

c.

Introduction (p. 422)

1. What is succession?

   _____

   _____

Primary Succession (p. 423)

2. What is primary succession?

   _____

   _____

   _____

Ecosystems • *Reading/Notetaking Guide*

Changes in Communities *(continued)*

3. Circle the letter of each choice that describes an area where primary succession might occur.

   a. a new island formed by the eruption of an undersea volcano
   b. an area of bare rock uncovered by a melting ice sheet
   c. a clearing in a forest left by cutting down the trees
   d. an area without any trees or other plants following a forest fire

4. The first species to populate the area in primary succession are called
   _____.

5. Primary species are often _____ and
   _____.

6. How do pioneer species help develop soil?
   _____

   _____

   _____

7. The particular species that come and go in the process of succession depend on the _____ of the area.

Secondary Succession (pp. 424–425)

8. The series of changes that occur where the ecosystem has been disturbed but soil and organisms still exist is called
   _____.

9. What natural disturbances can result in secondary succession?
   _____

   _____

10. What human activities can result in secondary succession?
   _____

   _____

11. Is the following sentence true or false? Secondary succession occurs more slowly than primary succession.
   _____

Biomes

Key Concepts

- What factors determine the type of biome found in an area?
- What are the characteristic organisms of the six major biomes?

A **biome** is a region with a certain climate and certain forms of vegetation. **It is mostly the climate—temperature and precipitation—in an area that determines its biome. The six major biomes are the desert, rain forest, grassland, deciduous forest, boreal forest, and tundra.** The climate limits distribution of plants. In turn, the types of plants determine the kinds of animals that live there.

A **desert** is an area that receives less than 25 centimeters of rain each year. Deserts have large shifts in temperature during the course of a day. Desert organisms are adapted to the lack of rain and to the extreme temperatures.

Tropical rain forests are warm and humid and found near the equator. The tall trees form a leafy roof called a **canopy.** A layer of shorter trees and vines forms an **understory.** Temperate rain forests are found farther north. They also receive a lot of rain but are cooler than tropical rain forests.

A **grassland** is an area that is populated mostly by grasses and other nonwoody plants. Most grasslands receive between 25 and 75 centimeters of rain each year and are populated mainly by grasses and other nonwoody plants. Grasslands that are located close to the equator are called **savannas.** Savannas receive as much as 120 centimeters of rain each year. Grasslands are home to many of the largest animals on Earth.

The trees found in deciduous forests, called **deciduous trees,** shed their leaves and grow new ones each year. These forests receive at least 50 centimeters of rain each year. Temperatures vary during the year. Some of the mammals enter a low-energy state called hibernation in the winter.

Boreal forests contain **coniferous trees,** which produce their seeds in cones and have leaves shaped like needles. Winters are long, very cold, and snowy. Summers are rainy and warm enough to melt all the snow.

The **tundra** is extremely cold and dry, often with no more precipitation than a desert. Most of the soil is frozen all year long. The frozen soil is called **permafrost.** Plants include low-growing mosses, grasses, and shrubs.

Some areas of land are not part of any major biome. These areas include land that is covered with thick sheets of ice and mountain ranges.

The climate changes dramatically as you go up a high mountain. Each altitude zone on the mountain has a different climate and a different community of plants. You would pass through different climate zones if you climbed from California's Central Valley to the top of a mountain in the Sierra Nevada.

Living Resources • *Reading/Notetaking Guide*

Biomes (pp. 438–447)

This section describes six major biomes, or regions with a certain climate and certain forms of vegetation. The section also tells where these different biomes are located.

Use Target Reading Skills

As you read, compare and contrast the different biomes by completing the table below.

	Temperature	Precipitation	Typical Organisms
Desert			
Tropical Rain Forest	Warm all year		
Temperate Rain Forest			
Grassland			
Deciduous Forest			
Boreal Forest			
Tundra			

Introduction (p. 438)

1. A region with a certain climate and certain form of vegetation is called a(n) _____.

2. Is the following sentence true or false? It is mostly the climate in an area that determines its biome. _____

Desert Biomes (p. 439)

3. Circle the letter of each sentence that is true about deserts.
   a. They receive less than 10 centimeters of rain per year.
   b. They have more evaporation than precipitation.
   c. They are always hot.
   d. They have extreme temperatures.

Rain Forest Biomes (pp. 440–441)

4. Circle the letter of each sentence that is true about tropical rain forests.
   a. They are found only in Africa and South America.
   b. They receive a lot of rainfall and sunlight year-round.
   c. They contain few species.
   d. They are much warmer in some seasons than in others.

5. The tall trees in a tropical rain forest form a leafy roof called the

   _____.

6. Compare and contrast the consumers in South American rain forests with those in Australian rain forests.

   _____

   _____

   _____

   _____

7. How do temperate rain forests differ from tropical rain forests?

   _____

   _____

   _____

Grassland Biomes (p. 442)

8. Circle the letter of each sentence that is true about grasslands.
   a. They have many trees.
   b. They have rich soil.
   c. They receive more than 75 centimeters of rain each year.
   d. They are home to many of the largest animals on Earth.

9. Grasslands that are located closer to the equator than prairies are called

   _____.

Living Resources · *Reading/Notetaking Guide*

Biomes (continued)

Deciduous Forest Biomes (p. 443)

10. Trees that shed their leaves and grow new ones each year are called

    _____.

11. Circle the letter of the sentence that is true about deciduous forests.
    a. They receive at least 50 centimeters of rain each year.
    b. Their temperatures are constant throughout the year.
    c. Their growing season usually lasts for 10 months.
    d. They contain very few habitats.

Boreal Forest Biomes (p. 444)

12. What type of trees are found in a boreal forest?

    _____

    _____

13. Circle the letter of each sentence that is true about boreal forests.
    a. They are farther north than deciduous forests.
    b. They have very cold winters.
    c. They receive little snow.
    d. Their most common species of trees are fir, spruce, and hemlock.

Tundra Biomes (p. 445)

14. An extremely cold, dry, land biome is the _____.

15. Circle the letter of each sentence that is true about the tundra.
    a. It may receive no more precipitation than a desert.
    b. Most of its soil is frozen all year.
    c. Its plants include mosses and dwarf trees.
    d. Its only animals are insects and birds.

Mountains and Ice (pp. 446–447)

16. Is the following sentence true or false? If you hiked to the top of a tall
    mountain, you would pass through different climate zones.

    _____

17. What are some organisms adapted to life on the ice?

    _____

    _____

Chapter 11 Living Resources • *Section 2 Summary*

Aquatic Ecosystems

Key Concepts

- What abiotic factors influence aquatic ecosystems?
- What are the major types of aquatic ecosystems?
- What are the ecological roles of organisms in aquatic food webs?

Almost three quarters of Earth's surface is covered with water. Many organisms make their homes in aquatic, or water-based, ecosystems. **All aquatic ecosystems are affected by the same abiotic factors: sunlight, temperature, oxygen, and salt content.**

Freshwater ecosystems include streams, rivers, ponds, and lakes. Animals that live in streams are adapted to the strong current. Few plants or algae grow in the fast-moving water of streams. As streams merge, they grow into larger, slower-moving rivers. Plants are able to root on river bottoms, and these producers provide food for young insects and homes for frogs and tadpoles.

Ponds and lakes are bodies of standing, or still, fresh water. Lakes are generally larger and deeper than ponds. In large ponds and most lakes, algae floating at the surface are the major producers. Many animals, including turtles, snails, dragonflies, frogs, and fish, are adapted to life in the still water of lakes and ponds. Scavengers such as catfish live near the bottom. Bacteria and other decomposers feed on the remains of other organisms.

The ocean has different zones. An **estuary** is found where the fresh water of a river meets the salt water of an ocean. **Marine ecosystems include estuaries, intertidal zones, neritic zones, and the open ocean. These zones are classified largely by the depth of water.** Between the highest high-tide line and the lowest low-tide line is the **intertidal zone.** Below the low-tide line is the **neritic zone,** a region of shallow water over the continental shelf. Below the open ocean's surface is the deep zone, which is completely dark.

Kelp forests, which occur off of California's coast, grow in cold neritic waters where the bottom is rocky. Giant kelp, a form of brown algae that grows up to 30 meters long, is the major producer in kelp forests. Kelp forests are home to many animals.

In tropical regions, coral reefs may form. **Coral reefs** are created by colonies of tiny coral animals. Incredible numbers of animals live in and around coral reefs, making them one of Earth's most diverse ecosystems.

As on land, organisms in the ocean are connected by food chains and food webs. But in the ocean, the producers are algae rather than plants. Most algae are **plankton**—tiny organisms that float in water. Throughout the ocean, plankton are a source of food for organisms of all sizes. For example, algae is eaten by single-celled consumers called protozoans. The protozoans are eaten by animal plankton, which are eaten by fish, which are eaten by top-level predators such as birds and seals.

Living Resources ▪ *Reading/Notetaking Guide*

Aquatic Ecosystems (pp. 450–455)

This section describes the major types of aquatic ecosystems. The section also tells what abiotic factors influence aquatic ecosystems and discusses aquatic food webs.

Use Target Reading Skills

Review the text in the second paragraph of the introduction to the section about aquatic ecosystems. Complete the chart below by identifying two important details about the main idea.

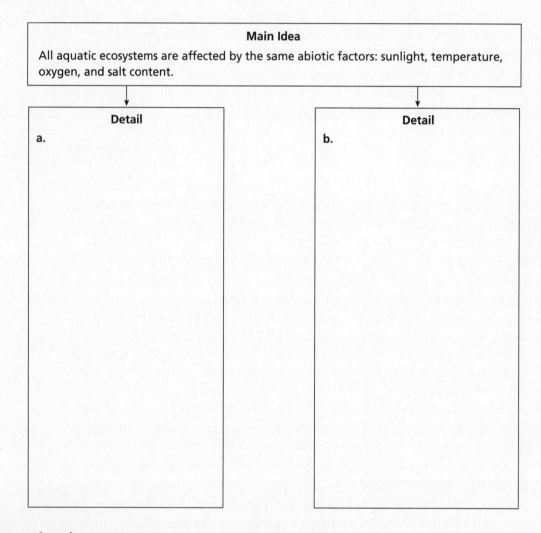

Main Idea

All aquatic ecosystems are affected by the same abiotic factors: sunlight, temperature, oxygen, and salt content.

Detail

a.

Detail

b.

Introduction (p. 450)

1. Is the following sentence true or false? Aquatic ecosystems are not affected by sunlight, temperature, oxygen, or salt content.

    _____

Freshwater Ecosystems (p. 451)

2. Is the following sentence true or false? Lakes are generally larger and deeper than ponds. _____

Living Resources · *Reading/Notetaking Guide*

3. Complete the Venn diagram.

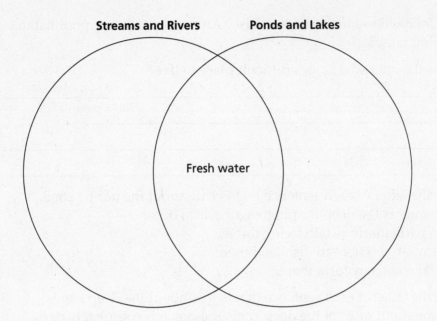

Streams and Rivers   Ponds and Lakes

Fresh water

4. What are some organisms adapted to life in a stream?

_____

_____

_____

Marine Ecosystems (pp. 452–453)

5. Complete the compare/contrast table.

Types of Marine Ecosystems	
Type of Biome	**Where It Is Located**
Estuary	Where fresh river water and salty ocean water meet
a.	Between the highest and lowest tide lines
b.	Below the low-tide line and out over the continental shelf
c.	On the surface of the open ocean
d.	Below the surface of the open ocean

Living Resources • *Reading/Notetaking Guide*

Aquatic Systems *(continued)*

6. Is the following sentence true or false? An estuary is a very poor habitat for living things. _____

7. Why is the intertidal zone a difficult place to live?

_____

_____

_____

_____

8. Circle the letter of each sentence that is true about the neritic zone.
   a. Its water is too deep for photosynthesis to occur.
   b. It is particularly rich in living things.
   c. Many large schools of fish feed there.
   d. Coral reefs may form there.

9. Circle the letter of each sentence that is true about the deep zone.
   a. Throughout most of the deep zone, the ocean is completely dark.
   b. Most animals in the deep zone feed on algae.
   c. Some animals in the deep zone have eyes that glow in the dark.
   d. Plants grow on the ocean floor in the deep zone.

Ocean Food Webs *(p. 454–455)*

10. Is the following sentence true or false? Algae form the basis of almost all open-ocean food webs. _____

11. Is the following sentence true or false? In the oceans, the producers are algae rather than plants. _____

12. Most algae are _____, tiny organisms that float in the water.

13. Circle the letter of each sentence that is true about ocean food webs.
   a. Single-celled consumers called protozoans eat much of the algae.
   b. Secondary consumers include jellyfish and worms.
   c. Fish are eaten by top-level predators such as birds and seals.
   d. There are no decomposers in an ocean food web.

Forests and Fisheries

Key Concepts

- How can forests be managed as renewable resources?
- How can fisheries be managed for a sustainable yield?

Forests are an important living resource. Trees and other plants produce oxygen that other organisms need. They also absorb carbon dioxide and many pollutants in the air. Forests help prevent flooding and control soil erosion. Many products come from forest plants. Because trees reproduce and grow relatively quickly, they are considered a renewable resource. A **renewable resource** is one that either is always available or is naturally replaced in a relatively short time.

Because new trees can be planted to replace trees that are cut down, forests can be renewable resources. There are two major methods of logging. Cutting down all the trees in an area at once is called **clear-cutting.** Cutting down only some trees and leaving a mix of tree sizes and species behind is called **selective cutting.** Clear-cutting is usually quicker and cheaper than selective cutting. However, selective cutting is usually less damaging to the forest environment. When an area of forest is clear-cut, the habitat changes. Clear-cutting also exposes the soil to wind and rain.

Forests can be managed to provide a sustainable yield. A **sustainable yield** is an amount of a renewable resource such as trees that can be harvested regularly without reducing the future supply. One sustainable approach is to log small patches of forest in stages. This way, different sections of forest can be harvested every year.

A **fishery** is an area with a large population of valuable ocean organisms. If a fishery is managed properly, it can be a valuable renewable resource. But if fish are caught at a faster rate than they can breed, the population decreases. This situation is called "overfishing."

Managing fisheries for a sustainable yield includes setting fishing limits, changing fishing methods, developing aquaculture techniques, and finding new resources. Laws can help protect fish species by limiting the total amount of fish that can be caught or by setting a minimum or maximum size for the fish. A fishery may be closed until the fish populations recover. Nets with larger holes can be used to allow young fish to escape. Fishing methods that kill all the fish in an area can be outlawed. **Aquaculture** is the practice of raising fish and other water-dwelling organisms for food. Another way to help feed a growing human population is to fish for new species.

Living Resources · *Reading/Notetaking Guide*

Forests and Fisheries (pp. 457–461)

This section describes resources that come from forests and from areas of the ocean called fisheries. The section also explains how forests and fisheries are managed to protect them for future use.

Use Target Reading Skills

Copy the outline below into your notebook. As you read about forests and fisheries, complete your outline. As you complete the outline, include main ideas, supporting details, and key terms.

<table>
<tr><td align="center">**Forests and Fisheries**</td></tr>
<tr><td>

   I. Forest Resources

  II. Managing Forests

     A. Logging Methods

     B. Sustainable Forestry

  III.

</td></tr>
</table>

Forest Resources (p. 457)

1. What are some valuable materials or products provided by forests?

_____

_____

2. Circle the letter of each sentence that is a reason people benefit from trees.
   a. Trees produce carbon dioxide.
   b. Trees absorb pollutants.
   c. Trees help prevent flooding.
   d. Trees help control soil erosion.

Living Resources • *Reading/Notetaking Guide*

Managing Forests (pp. 457–461)

3. Is the following sentence true or false? Nearly a third of the area of the United States is covered with forests. _____

4. Is the following sentence true or false? Forests contain no valuable resources. _____

5. Complete the Venn diagram.

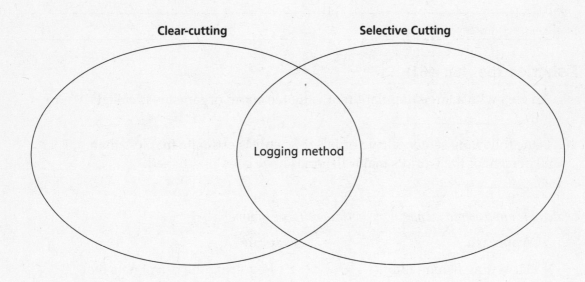

Clear-cutting   Selective Cutting

Logging method

6. Complete the compare/contrast table.

Advantages and Disadvantages of Different Logging Methods		
Logging Method	**Advantages**	**Disadvantages**
a.	Quicker, cheaper, safer	Exposes soil to erosion
b.	Less damaging to habitat	Can be dangerous to loggers

Living Resources · *Reading/Notetaking Guide*

Forests and Fisheries *(continued)*

7. A regular amount of a renewable resource that can be harvested without reducing the future supply is called a(n) _____.

8. How can forests provide a sustainable yield?

_____

_____

_____

_____

Fisheries (pp. 460–461)

9. An area with a large population of valuable ocean organisms is called a(n) _____.

10. Is the following sentence true or false? Scientists estimate that less than 50 percent of the world's major fisheries have been overfished. _____

Match the approach to managing fisheries with its example.

Approach	Example
____ 11. setting fishing limits	**a.** Requiring the use of nets that allow young fish to escape
____ 12. changing fishing methods	
____ 13. developing aquaculture techniques	**b.** Introducing new species of fish as food
____ 14. finding new resources	**c.** Setting an upper limit on the amount of fish that can be caught
	d. Raising fish in an artificial pond

Biodiversity

Key Concepts

- In what ways is biodiversity valuable?

- What factors affect an area's biodiversity?

- Which human activities threaten biodiversity?

- How can biodiversity be protected?

The number of different species in an area is called its **biodiversity.** Preserving biodiversity is important. **People value wildlife and ecosystems for their beauty and as a source of recreation. In addition, biodiversity has both economic value and ecological value within an ecosystem.** Organisms also provide food, oxygen, and raw materials for clothing, medicine, and other products. All the species in an ecosystem are connected to one another.

Factors that affect biodiversity in an ecosystem include area, climate, and diversity of niches. Tropical rain forests are the most diverse ecosystems in the world. The climate makes food available for organisms year-round. Coral reefs are the second most diverse ecosystems in the world. A reef provides many different niches for organisms. A species that influences the survival of many other species in an ecosystem is called a **keystone species**.

The disappearance of all members of a species from Earth is called **extinction.** Species in danger of becoming extinct in the near future are considered **endangered species.** Species that could become endangered in the near future are considered **threatened species.** Natural events such as earthquakes can cause species to become extinct. **Human activities can also threaten biodiversity. These activities include habitat destruction, poaching, pollution, and the introduction of nonnative species.** The major cause of extinction is **habitat destruction,** the loss of a natural habitat. The illegal killing or removal of wildlife from their habitats is called **poaching.** Some species are endangered because pollutants build up in organisms through the food chain. Introducing exotic species into an ecosystem can also threaten biodiversity.

Three successful approaches to protecting biodiversity are captive breeding, laws and treaties, and habitat preservation. One scientific approach is **captive breeding,** which is the mating of animals in zoos or wildlife preserves. Laws and treaties can help protect species by making it illegal to sell endangered species or products made from them. The most effective way to preserve biodiversity is to protect whole ecosystems.

Living Resources · *Reading/Notetaking Guide*

Biodiversity (pp. 462–467)

This section describes factors that affect biodiversity, or the number of species in an area. The section also explains why biodiversity is valuable, how it is being threatened, and what is being done to protect it.

Use Target Reading Skills

Review the paragraphs under the heading "Factors Affecting Biodiversity." Complete the chart below by identifying three important details about the main idea.

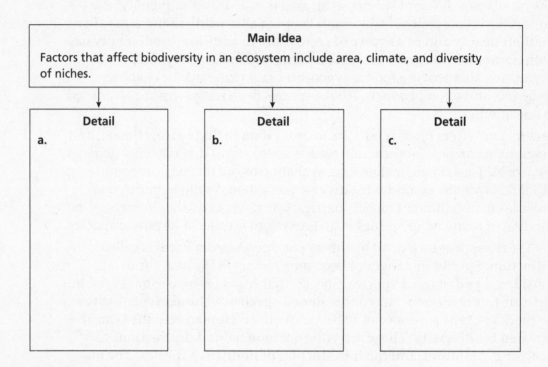

Main Idea

Factors that affect biodiversity in an ecosystem include area, climate, and diversity of niches.

Detail	**Detail**	**Detail**
a.	b.	c.

Introduction (p. 462)

1. The number of different species in an area is called its

   _____.

2. Is the following sentence true or false? Biodiversity has no economic value. _____

Factors Affecting Biodiversity (p. 463)

3. A species that influences the survival of many other species in an ecosystem is called a(n) _____.

4. Is the following sentence true or false? If a keystone species disappears, the entire ecosystem may change. _____

Living Resources · *Reading/Notetaking Guide*

5. Complete the concept map.

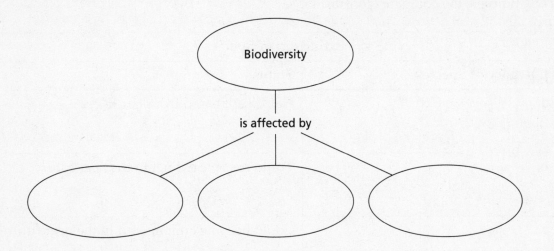

6. Circle the letter of each sentence that is true about biodiversity.
   a. Large areas contain more species than small areas.
   b. The number of species decreases from the poles toward the equator.
   c. Tropical rain forests are the most diverse ecosystems.
   d. Coral reefs are the second most diverse ecosystems.

7. What is niche diversity?

   _____

   _____

   _____

Biodiversity in Danger (pp. 464–465)

8. The disappearance of all members of a species from Earth is called

   _____.

9. Circle the letter of each sentence that is true about extinction.
   a. It is a natural process.
   b. Many species are now extinct.
   c. Extinctions have occurred only in the last few centuries.
   d. The number of species becoming extinct has increased dramatically.

10. Is the following sentence true or false? Threatened and endangered
    species are found on every continent and in every ocean.

    _____

Living Resources • *Reading/Notetaking Guide*

Biodiversity (continued)

11. Complete the compare/contrast table.

Extinction of Species	
Category of Species	Status
a.	Has disappeared from Earth
b.	Could become extinct in the near future
c.	Could become endangered in the near future

12. What natural events might cause extinction?

_____

_____

13. Is the following sentence true or false? The major cause of extinction is habitat destruction. _____

Match the term with its definition.

Term

____ **14.** habitat destruction

____ **15.** invasive species

____ **16.** poaching

Definition

a. A nonnative species

b. Illegally killing or removing wildlife from their habitats

c. Loss of a natural habitat

17. How can pollutants affect organisms?

_____

_____

Protecting Biodiversity (pp. 466–467)

18. The mating of animals in zoos or wildlife preserves to protect severely endangered species is called _____.

19. Is the following sentence true or false? Laws can help protect individual species. _____

20. Is this sentence true or false? The most effective way to preserve biodiversity is to protect individual species. _____

Chapter 12 Energy and Material Resources • *Section 1 Summary*

Fossil Fuels

Key Concepts

■ How do fuels provide energy?

■ What are the three major fossil fuels?

■ Why are fossil fuels considered nonrenewable resources?

A **fuel** is a substance that provides a form of energy—such as heat, light, electricity, or motion—as the result of a chemical change. This change from one form of energy to another is called **energy transformation. When fuels are burned, chemical energy is released as heat and light. These forms of energy can be used to generate other forms of energy, such as motion or electricity.** The process of burning a fuel is called **combustion.**

Most of the energy used today comes from fossil fuels. **Fossil fuels** are the energy-rich substances formed from the remains of once-living organisms. Layers of sand, rock, and mud buried the dead organisms. Over millions of years, heat and pressure changed the materials into fossil fuels. **The three major fossil fuels are coal, oil, and natural gas.** Fossil fuels are made of hydrocarbons. **Hydrocarbons** are energy-rich chemical compounds that contain carbon and hydrogen.

Coal is a solid fossil fuel formed from decaying plant matter. Known deposits of coal and other fossil fuels that can be obtained using current technology are called reserves. Coal is the most plentiful fossil fuel in the United States. It is fairly easy to transport and provides a lot of energy when it is burned. However, coal mining can cause erosion and water pollution. When burned, most types of coal cause more air pollution than other fossil fuels. In addition, coal mining can be a dangerous job.

Oil is a thick, black liquid fossil fuel. **Petroleum** is another name for oil. Oil is formed from the remains of small ocean-living organisms. Most oil deposits are located deep below Earth's surface. Oil that is pumped out of the ground is called crude oil. A factory where crude oil is separated into fuels and other products by heating is called a **refinery. Petrochemicals** are compounds that are made from oil.

Natural gas is a mixture of methane and other gases. Natural gas forms from the same organisms as oil. Because it is less dense than oil, natural gas often rises above an oil deposit, forming a pocket. Natural gas produces lower levels of many air pollutants than coal or oil and is fairly easy to transport. However, natural gas is highly flammable. A gas leak can cause a violent explosion and fire.

People currently rely very heavily on fossil fuels. **But since fossil fuels take hundreds of millions of years to form, they are considered nonrenewable resources.** Fossil fuels are being used at a faster rate than they are formed. New sources of energy are needed to replace the decreasing fossil fuel reserves.

Energy and Material Resources ▪ *Reading/Notetaking Guide*

Fossil Fuels (pp. 478–484)

This section explains how fuels provide energy. The section also explains what fossil fuels are and compares and contrasts the different types of fossil fuels.

Use Target Reading Skills

As you read about the three major types of fossil fuels, complete the compare-and-contrast table below.

Type	How Formed	Renewable or Nonrenewable?
a.	From ancient plant remains	b.
Oil	c.	Nonrenewable
d.	From the remains of small ocean organisms	e.

Energy Transformation and Fuels (pp. 478–479)

1. A substance that provides a form of energy, such as heat, as a result of a chemical change is a(n) _____.

2. Is the following sentence true or false? Energy cannot be converted from one form to another. _____

3. The process of burning a fuel is called _____.

4. Is the following sentence true or false? The energy stored in fuels can be used to generate electricity. _____

5. Circle the letter of each sentence that is true about the production of electric power.
   a. In most power plants, water is boiled to make steam.
   b. The mechanical energy of steam turns the shaft of a generator.
   c. Powerful magnets turn inside a wire coil.
   d. Electricity is produced by a turbine.

What Are Fossil Fuels? (p. 480)

6. Energy-rich substances formed from the remains of once-living organisms are called _____.

7. List the three major fossil fuels.

   a. _____ b. _____

   c. _____

Energy and Material Resources ▪ *Reading/Notetaking Guide*

8. Chemical compounds that contain carbon and hydrogen are called
_____.

9. Complete the flowchart.

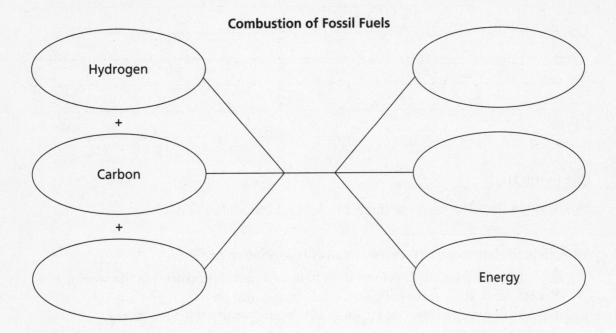

Combustion of Fossil Fuels

Coal (pp. 480–481)

10. A solid fossil fuel formed from plant remains is

_____.

11. Is the following sentence true or false? Today, coal provides about 23 percent of the energy used in the United States. _____

12. Is the following sentence true or false? The major use of coal in the United States is to fuel factories. _____

13. Circle the letter of the sentence that is true about coal as an energy source.
    a. It is the least plentiful fossil fuel in the United States.
    b. It is difficult to transport.
    c. It provides a lot of energy when burned.
    d. It produces less air pollution than other fossil fuels.

Energy and Material Resources ▪ *Reading/Notetaking Guide*

Fossil Fuels (continued)

14. How can coal mining harm the environment?

_____

_____

_____

_____

_____

_____

Oil (p. 482)

15. Another name for oil—the thick, black, liquid fossil fuel—is

_____.

16. Circle the letter of each sentence that is true about petroleum.

   a. Petroleum accounts for more than half the energy produced in the world.
   b. Petroleum fuels most cars, airplanes, trains, and ships.
   c. The discovery of new oil supplies is keeping steady with the use of existing supplies.
   d. Finding oil is difficult.

17. What kinds of rocks are oil deposits most commonly found in?

_____

18. When oil is first pumped out of the ground, it is called

_____.

19. A factory where crude oil is separated into fuels and other products by heating is called a(n) _____.

20. Compounds that are made from oil are called

_____.

Natural Gas (p. 483)

21. Circle the letter of each sentence that is true about natural gas.

   a. It is a fossil fuel.
   b. It produces more air pollution than oil.
   c. It cannot be transported by pipelines.
   d. It is highly flammable.

22. Is the following sentence true or false? Because natural gas is less dense than oil, it often rises above an oil deposit. _____

Energy and Material Resources ▪ *Reading/Notetaking Guide*

Fuel Supply and Demand (p. 484)

23. Is the following sentence true or false? Fossil fuels are considered a renewable resource. _____

24. Circle the letter of each sentence that is true about the supply of fossil fuels.

    a. Fossil fuels take hundreds of millions of years to form.
    b. The United States has to buy a lot of oil from other countries.
    c. New supplies of oil and natural gas are being found faster than they are being used up.
    d. New sources of energy are needed to replace decreasing fossil fuel reserves.

Chapter 12 Energy and Material Resources • *Section 2 Summary*

Renewable Sources of Energy

Key Concepts

- What forms of energy does the sun provide?

- What are some renewable sources of energy?

Solar energy is energy from the sun. **The sun constantly gives off energy in the forms of light and heat.** Solar energy is the source, directly or indirectly, of most other renewable energy resources. In a solar power plant, giant mirrors focus the sun's rays to boil water. The steam can be used to generate electricity. Solar energy also can be converted directly into electricity in a solar cell. Solar energy can be used to heat homes and other buildings. A passive solar system converts sunlight into thermal energy without using pumps or fans. An active solar system captures the sun's energy, then uses fans and pumps to distribute the heat.

    Other renewable sources of energy include water, the wind, biomass fuels, geothermal energy, and the tides. Solar energy is also the indirect source of water power. The sun drives the water cycle. Flowing water can turn a turbine and generate electricity. Electricity produced by flowing water is called **hydroelectric power.** Once the dam and power plant are built, hydroelectric power is inexpensive and clean. However, in the United States, most suitable rivers have already been dammed. Also, dams can have negative effects on the environment.

    Wind power is also a renewable energy resource. Large wind farms contain many wind turbines. The turbines turn to generate electricity. Wind power causes no pollution and is renewable. It is possibly the fastest-growing energy resource. Drawbacks of using wind power include the need for steady strong winds and opposition to the building of wind farms in scenic areas.

    Fuels made from material that was once part of a living thing are called **biomass fuels.** Examples include wood, leaves, food wastes, and manure. Burning these fuels releases energy. Biomass materials can also be converted into other fuels, such as alcohol. Adding the alcohol to gasoline forms a mixture called **gasohol.** Currently it is expensive to produce biomass fuels in large quantities.

    The intense heat from Earth's interior that warms magma is called **geothermal energy.** The magma heats underground water, and the steam can be used to heat homes and generate electricity. However, magma is close to Earth's surface in only a few places. In other areas, expensive deep wells would be needed to tap this energy.

    Another source of moving water is the tides. **Tides** are the regular rise and fall of Earth's waters along its shores. Along coastlines, water flows into and out of bays as tides come in and go out. Tidal power plants use this regular flow to turn turbines and generate electricity. However, only a few places on Earth are suitable for tidal power plants.

Energy and Material Resources • *Reading/Notetaking Guide*

Renewable Sources of Energy (pp. 485–491)

This section describes several renewable sources of energy and explains the advantages and disadvantages of each energy source.

Use Target Reading Skills

As you read about the four ways to capture solar energy, complete the compare-and-contrast table below.

Solar Energy Source	How It Works
Solar power plants	a.
Solar cells	b.
Passive solar heating	c.
Active solar heating	d.

Harnessing the Sun's Energy (pp. 486–487)

1. What is solar energy?

   _____

   _____

   _____

2. Circle the letter of each sentence that is true about solar energy.

   a. It is the source of most other renewable energy resources.
   b. It causes a lot of pollution.
   c. It will not run out for billions of years.
   d. It is available only when the sun is shining.

3. How do solar power plants capture solar energy and use it to generate electricity?

   _____

   _____

4. Is the following sentence true or false? Solar energy can be converted directly into electricity in a solar cell. _____

Energy and Material Resources • *Reading/Notetaking Guide*

Renewable Sources of Energy *(continued)*

5. What are some small devices that solar cells are used to power?

_____

_____

6. Is the following sentence true or false? Passive solar heating systems convert sunlight into electricity. _____

7. Complete the concept map.

```
        ╭─────────────────────╮
        │  Solar heating systems │
        ╰─────────────────────╯
                  │
               can be
              /        \
     ╭──────────╮    ╭──────────╮
     │          │    │          │
     ╰──────────╯    ╰──────────╯
```

8. How do active solar heating systems differ from passive solar heating systems?

_____

_____

_____

_____

Hydroelectric Power (p. 488)

9. List other renewable sources of energy besides the sun.

a. _____ b. _____

c. _____ d. _____

e. _____

10. Electricity produced by flowing water is called

_____ .

Energy and Material Resources ▪ *Reading/Notetaking Guide*

11. Is the following sentence true or false? Hydroelectric power is the least widely used source of renewable energy in the world today.

    _____

12. What are two limitations on hydroelectric power in the United States?

    _____

    _____

    _____

Wind Power (pp. 488–489)

13. Circle the letter of each sentence that is true about wind energy.

    a. Wind farms consist of a single wind turbine.
    b. Wind energy is perhaps the fastest-growing energy resource.
    c. Wind energy causes much pollution.
    d. People may object to windmills being built in scenic areas.

14. Is the following sentence true or false? Most places have winds that blow steadily enough to be a worthwhile energy source.

    _____

Biomass Fuels (p. 489)

15. Fuels made from material that was once part of a living thing are called

    _____.

16. Circle the letter of each sentence that is true about biomass fuels.

    a. They include leaves, food wastes, and manure.
    b. They can be converted to other fuels.
    c. They are widely used today in the United States.
    d. They are renewable resources.

Tapping Earth's Energy (p. 490)

17. Intense heat from Earth's interior is called _____.

18. Is the following sentence true or false? Geothermal energy can be used to heat homes or generate electricity in certain regions.

    _____

Renewable Sources of Energy *(continued)*

19. Add arrows to the drawing to show how water flows through a geothermal power plant.

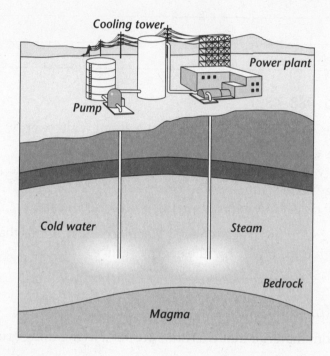

Tidal Energy *(p. 491)*

20. Circle the letter of each sentence that is true about tidal energy.

    a. A large difference between high and low tide is necessary.
    b. Tidal energy relies on the regular rise and fall of Earth's oceans.
    c. Energy is generated as water flows in both directions.
    d. Tidal energy is a practical energy source in many regions.

21. What is a limitation of using tidal energy?

    _____

    _____

    _____

    _____

Chapter 12 Energy and Material Resources • *Section 3 Summary*

Nuclear Energy

Key Concepts

- What happens during a nuclear fission reaction?
- How does a nuclear power plant produce electricity?
- How does a nuclear fusion reaction occur?

The **nucleus** is the central core of an atom that contains the protons and neutrons. **Nuclear fission** is the splitting of an atom's nucleus into two smaller nuclei. The fuel for the reaction is a large atom that has an unstable nucleus, such as uranium-235. A neutron is shot at the U-235 atom at high speed. **When the neutron hits the U-235 nucleus, the nucleus splits apart into two smaller nuclei and two or more neutrons.** The total mass of all these particles is a bit less than the mass of the original nucleus. The small amount of mass that makes up the difference has been converted into energy. The process continues over and over in a chain reaction. If a nuclear chain reaction is not controlled, the released energy produces a huge explosion. If the chain reaction is controlled, the energy is released as heat, which can be used to generate electricity.

In a nuclear power plant, the heat energy released from fission is used to change water into steam. The steam then turns the blades of a turbine to generate electricity. The **reactor vessel** is the section of a nuclear reactor where nuclear fission occurs. The reactor contains rods of uranium, called **fuel rods.** The chain reaction is controlled by placing **control rods** made of the metal cadmium between the fuel rods. The heat that is produced is used to boil water to produce steam, which runs the electrical generator.

Nuclear power plants have some problems. If the fuel rods generate too much heat, they start to melt, a condition called a **meltdown.** This can cause an explosion. Also, radioactive wastes produced by nuclear power plants remain dangerous for thousands of years. Finding a place to safely store these wastes is very difficult. Nuclear power plants emit large amounts of heat. However, they don't pollute the air.

A second type of nuclear reaction is fusion. **Nuclear fusion** is the combining of two atomic nuclei to produce a single larger nucleus. **In nuclear fusion, two hydrogen nuclei combine to create a helium nucleus, which has slightly less mass than the two hydrogen nuclei. The lost mass is converted to large amounts of energy.**

Nuclear fusion is a promising future energy source. The fuel for a fusion reaction could be obtained from water. Fusion would not produce air pollution or long-lived radioactive wastes. But fusion can take place only at extremely high temperatures and pressures. Scientists have not yet found a way to build a large-scale fusion reactor.

Energy and Material Resources • *Reading/Notetaking Guide*

Nuclear Energy (pp. 494–498)

This section explains how nuclear reactions inside atoms can produce energy. The section also describes the advantages and disadvantages of nuclear energy.

Use Target Reading Skills

As you read, compare and contrast fission and fusion reactions in the Venn diagram below. Write the similarities in the space where the circles overlap and the differences on the left and right sides.

Nuclear Fission   **Nuclear Fusion**

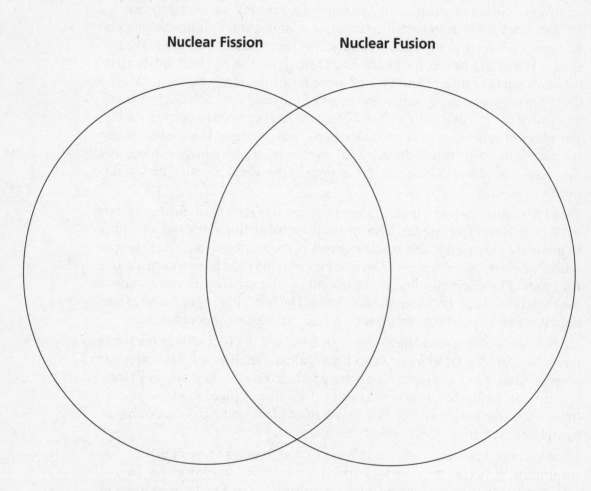

Energy and Material Resources ▪ *Reading/Notetaking Guide*

Introduction (p. 494)

1. The central core of an atom that contains the protons and neutrons is called the _____.

2. Complete the concept map.

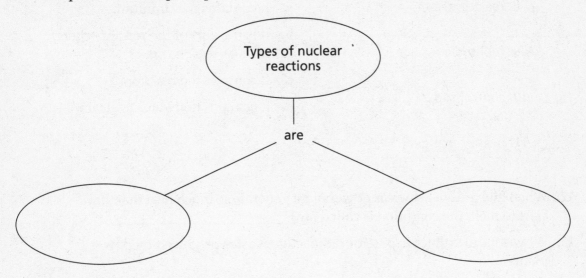

Nuclear Fission (pp. 494–495)

3. Is the following sentence true or false? Nuclear reactions convert matter into energy. _____

4. What formula, developed by Albert Einstein, describes the relationship between energy and matter?

    _____

5. The splitting of an atom's nucleus into two smaller nuclei is called

    _____.

6. Is the following sentence true or false? In a controlled nuclear chain reaction, the energy released as heat can be used to generate electricity.

    _____

Nuclear Power Plants (pp. 496–497)

7. How is electricity produced in a nuclear power plant?

    _____

    _____

    _____

    _____

    _____

Name _____ Date _____ Class _____

Energy and Material Resources • *Reading/Notetaking Guide*

Nuclear Energy (continued)

Match the part of a nuclear reactor with its function.

Part of Reactor	Function
____ **8.** reactor vessel	**a.** It contains the uranium.
____ **9.** fuel rod	**b.** It is the part of the reactor where nuclear fission occurs.
____ **10.** control rod	**c.** It controls the reactions.
	d. It changes hot water to steam.
____ **11.** heat exchanger	

12. When fuel rods in a nuclear power plant generate so much heat that they start to melt, the condition is called a(n) _____.

13. Why is it difficult to dispose of radioactive wastes produced by power plants?

_____

_____

_____

_____

The Quest to Control Fusion (p. 498)

14. The combining of two atomic nuclei to produce a single larger nucleus is called _____.

15. Circle the letter of each sentence that is true about nuclear fusion.

a. It is considered a nonrenewable energy source.

b. The fuel it needs is readily available.

c. It will not produce long-lived radioactive waste.

d. It is widely used today to produce electricity.

Energy Conservation

Key Concept

■ What are two ways to preserve our current energy sources?

Fossil fuels will not last forever. Most people think that it makes sense to start planning now to avoid possible fuel shortages in the future. **One way to preserve energy resources is to increase the efficiency of energy use. Another way is to conserve energy whenever possible.**

One way to get as much work as possible out of fuels is to use them efficiently. **Efficiency** is the percentage of energy that is actually used to perform work. The rest of the energy is "lost" to the surroundings, usually as heat. For example, an incandescent light bulb converts only about 10 percent of the electricity it uses into light. The rest is given off as heat. In contrast, a compact fluorescent bulb uses only about one fourth as much energy to provide the same amount of light.

One method of increasing the efficiency of heating and cooling systems is insulation. **Insulation** is a layer of material that traps air to help block the transfer of heat between the air inside and outside a building.

Engineers have improved the efficiency of cars by designing better engines and tires. Another way to save energy is to use public transit systems and carpool. In the future, cars that run on electricity may provide the most energy savings of all.

Reducing energy use is called **energy conservation.** For example, walking to the store instead of driving a car conserves gasoline. You can even reduce your personal energy use. Instead of turning up the heat, put on a sweater. When the weather is hot, use fans instead of air conditioners.

Energy and Material Resources ▪ *Reading/Notetaking Guide*

Energy Conservation (pp. 499–502)

This section describes several ways that energy use can be reduced to make available fuels last as long as possible.

Use Target Reading Skills

Preview the red heading Energy Efficiency *and the blue subheadings* Heating and Cooling, Lighting, *and* Transportation. *Complete the graphic organizer below by answering the question that is asked about each heading.*

Heading	Question	Answer
Heating and Cooling	What is insulation?	a.
Lighting	Which type of bulb is more efficient, incandescent or fluorescent?	b.
Transportation	How can the number of cars on the road be reduced?	c.

Introduction (p. 499)

1. What are two ways to preserve our current energy sources?

   _____

   _____

   _____

   _____

   _____

Energy and Material Resources ▪ *Reading/Notetaking Guide*

Energy Efficiency (pp. 500–501)

2. The percentage of energy from a fuel that is actually used to perform work is its _____.

3. What happens to the energy from a fuel that is not used to perform work?

   _____

   _____

   _____

   _____

4. A layer of material that helps block the transfer of heat between the air inside and the air outside a building is called _____.

5. How does insulation work?

   _____

   _____

   _____

   _____

   _____

6. Circle the letter of the choice that is the most common material used for insulation.
   a. fiberglass
   b. brick
   c. stone
   d. glass

7. Why do new windows often have two panes of glass with space between them?

   _____

   _____

   _____

   _____

Energy and Material Resources • *Reading/Notetaking Guide*

Energy Conservation *(continued)*

8. Is the following sentence true or false? Incandescent light bulbs waste less energy than compact fluorescent bulbs. _____

9. How have engineers improved the energy efficiency of cars?

_____

_____

_____

_____

_____

10. What are some ways to reduce the number of cars on the road?

_____

_____

_____

_____

_____

Energy Conservation (p. 502)

11. Reducing energy use is called _____.

12. Circle the letter of each sentence that describes a way you can reduce your personal energy use.

   a. Use air conditioners instead of fans.
   b. Use electric lights whenever possible.
   c. Walk or ride a bike for short trips.
   d. Recycle.

Recycling Material Resources

Key Concepts

■ What are three methods of handling solid waste?

■ What can people do to help control the solid waste problem?

The waste materials produced in homes, businesses, schools, and other places in a community are called **municipal solid waste.** Other sources of solid waste include construction debris and certain agricultural and industrial wastes. **Three methods of handling solid waste are burning, burying, and recycling. Each method has advantages and disadvantages.**

The burning of solid waste is called **incineration.** The advantages are that incinerators do not take up much space, and the heat produced by burning solid waste can be used to generate electricity. The disadvantages are that incinerators do release some pollution into the air, some waste still remains after incineration, and incinerators are expensive to build.

Disposing of solid waste in open dumps is dangerous because rainwater dissolves chemicals from the waste. This polluted liquid, called **leachate,** can run off into streams and rivers or trickle down into the groundwater. Today, much solid waste is buried in landfills that hold the waste more safely. A **sanitary landfill** holds municipal solid waste, construction debris, and some types of agricultural and industrial waste. Even well-designed landfills can pose a risk of polluting groundwater.

The process of reclaiming raw materials and reusing them to create new products is called **recycling.** Recycling reduces the volume of solid waste by enabling people to use the materials in wastes again. Any material that can be broken down and recycled by bacteria and other decomposers is **biodegradable.** Unfortunately, many of the products people use today are not biodegradable. Instead, people have developed techniques to recycle the raw materials in these products. Most recycling focuses on four major categories of products: metal, plastic, glass, and paper.

There are ways individuals can help control the solid waste problem. **These are sometimes called the "three R's"—reduce, reuse, and recycle.** *Reduce* refers to creating less waste in the first place. *Reuse* refers to finding another use for an object rather than discarding it. *Recycle* refers to reclaiming raw materials to create new products. Another way to reduce the amount of solid waste is by composting. **Composting** is the process of helping biodegradable wastes to decompose naturally.

Energy and Material Resources · *Reading/Notetaking Guide*

Recycling Material Resources (pp. 506–511)

This section explains what solid waste is, where it comes from, how solid waste is handled, and how individuals can help control solid waste.

Use Target Reading Skills

Complete the first column in the chart by filling in the red headings. Then in the second column, ask a what, how, *or* where *question for each heading. As you read the section, complete the third column with the answers.*

Section 5: Recycling Material Resources		
Heading	**Quesiton**	**Answer**

The Problem of Waste Disposal (pp. 507–508)

1. What is municipal solid waste?

   _____

   _____

   _____

2. What are other sources of solid waste?

   _____

   _____

   _____

Energy and Material Resources ▪ *Reading/Notetaking Guide*

3. List three methods of handling solid waste.

   a. _____ b. _____

   c. _____

4. Circle the letter of each sentence that is true about incineration.

   a. It refers to the burning of solid waste.
   b. It can be used to generate electricity.
   c. It gets rid of solid waste completely.
   d. Incinerators do not pollute the air.

5. A place where solid waste is buried is called a(n)

   _____.

6. A polluted liquid that forms when rainwater dissolves chemicals in landfill waste is referred to as _____.

7. How does a sanitary landfill differ from an open dump?

   _____

   _____

   _____

   _____

8. Label each circle in the Venn diagram with the method of solid waste management it represents.

   a. _____   b. _____

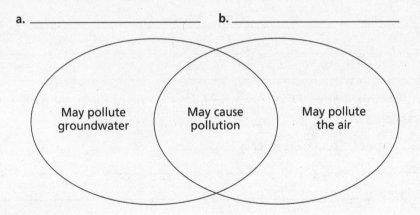

May pollute groundwater   May cause pollution   May pollute the air

© Pearson Education, Inc. All rights reserved.

Energy and Material Resources • *Reading/Notetaking Guide*

Recycling Material Resources *(continued)*

Recycling *(pp. 509–510)*

9. What is recycling?

   _____

   _____

   _____

10. Is the following sentence true or false? Recycling reduces the volume of solid waste. _____

11. A substance that can be broken down and recycled by bacteria and other decomposers is said to be _____.

12. List the four major categories of products that are recycled.

    a. _____ b. _____

    c. _____ d. _____

13. What are some common plastic objects that can be recycled?

    _____

    _____

    _____

14. What products can be made from recycled plastic milk jugs and soda bottles?

    _____

    _____

    _____

15. Is the following sentence true or false? Glass is one of the most difficult products to recycle. _____

16. Why can paper be recycled only a few times?

    _____

    _____

    _____

17. Circle the letter of each sentence that is true about recycling.

    a. It conserves resources.
    b. It can be done easily for all materials.
    c. It saves energy.
    d. It can be used for all types of solid waste.

Energy and Material Resources ▪ *Reading/Notetaking Guide*

What People Can Do (p. 511)

18. Complete the concept map.

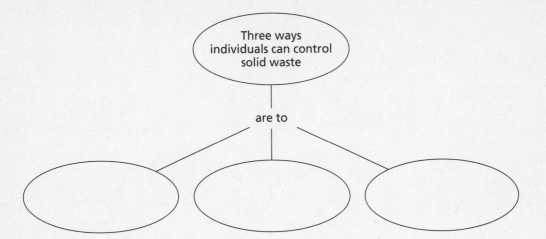

19. Helping natural decomposition processes break down waste is called
_____.

20. How can compost be used?

_____

_____

_____

_____

_____

_____